Distributive Justice
and Fair Exchange

Distributive Justice
and
Fair Exchange

How to find and use social standards

Emanuel Smikun

AMINSO
Peabody, Massachusetts

Distributive Justice and Fair Exchange

Published by: AMINSO
300 Andover Street, Suite 157
Peabody, MA 01960

Printed in the United States of America

EAN13: 978-0983702511
ISBN: 0983702519

Library of Congress Control Number: 2011907116

Contents

1

Status and Class Exchange

As members of organized groups and society at large, we engage in meaningful social action to correct prevailing conditions that we consider unsatisfactory or unfair. Yet our knowledge of such conditions is often unreliable and erroneous. It usually consists of impressionistic news headlines and stories reflecting social myths and yesteryear ideologies. What we believe is a just cause may reflect fiction rather than fact. Even when such knowledge is obtained with the help of a social-scientific method, it may be misleading. Many observers note that old formulas and approaches no longer apply. Classic economic theory was shaken by Marxism a century and a half ago, and again by Keynes following the Great Depression. If history is any teacher, the current worldwide socioeconomic upheaval may force us to change fundamental beliefs about our social world and about our best practices aimed at its improvement.

More than a century ago Max Weber deliberated about the possibility of socio-economic policies based on valid standards derived from critical value judgments of empirical facts. He also recognized the need for a rational understanding of social values involved in such value judgments. Weber's reflections on this subject matter are now a standard text in sociological theory and methodology. This shows, incidentally, that we have not progressed substantially in the endeavor for a practical social science. Weber's appeal still remains in the realm of the old philosophical debates about the possibility of deriving "ought" from "is". We are good at empirical observation of social conditions and of public opinion. Huge amounts of empirical facts have been accumulated. But how can we obtain normative standards from "objectively valid" critical evaluations of all these facts? And what values are relevant in social policies that such standards should invoke?

From Atomized Individuals
to Social Groups

Today as in Weber's time, the answer to this latter question lies on the very surface of our public life. Movements for social justice are sweeping the world, and social scientists should be primarily concerned about that. But what do we mean by social justice now that the welfare state has outlived its time of post-Great Depression emergency? Where do our standards of social justice originate? Do we have a rational understanding of its ideologically charged principles? Is recycling yesteryear opposing ideologies sufficient? And is social justice compatible with progressive and sustainable social development? Can the social sciences be more helpful? In his 2004 presidential address to the American Sociological Association and in numerous printed publications, Michael Burawoy called for a translation of the "impressive body of theory, empirical analysis, and innovative techniques" developed by sociologists over the last one hundred years back into a language meaningful to the public. It was this service to the public that inspired the growth of professional sociology in the first place.

The interpenetration between sociology and economics is in vogue. The notion of embeddedness of economic phenomena in social institutions is widely accepted. It has been popular for a quarter of a century now. [1] Embeddedness is a good general epistemological orientation for economic sociology, but do we have to stop at that? Economics studies production, distribution, exchange and consumption of limited material resources ranging from oil and gold to water. We can do better than that. While recognizing that economics is a more developed and more established discipline, and that sociology has much to learn from some of its central concepts, we can still keep the sociological subject-matter *sui generis*. Rather than studying embeddedness of standard items of economists' subject-matter such as shopping and consumer preferences, we can begin by finding the sociological meanings of some of economics' key concepts as the classics of sociology did in their time.

The first concept that comes to mind is exchange as a mechanism of achieving the ideal of distributive social justice. Economics is based on the view of social reality as a mass society of rational individuals. This view is deceptive. The view of society consisting of distinct groups of people of different kind - rather than individuals and corporations with government controlling them - conforms better to the ideal of a commonwealth, or a republic in its ancient sense of common cause (the Roman *res publica*). Basic to the notion of a commonwealth is self-government of multiple social groups. In a commonwealth, social justice is not the result of free and arbitrary competition of individual wills, nor is it the result of a benevolent central government providing welfare for the individuals collected in a society - like a father taking care of his immature children. Neither corporations nor central government are capable of bringing social justice with the system of restorative law enforcement for individuals. Social justice is primarily a matter of fair relations among groups of people, and it is only possible in a commonwealth of active self-governing status groups pursuing shared class interests.

We are surrounded by an overwhelming variety of things that noisily command our attention on television, the internet, and other mass communication media. The idea is to see them only as particular representations or indicators of common social meanings rather than as gratification of individual wants. It is the meaning of things standing for structures of human social relations that is important here. [2] What is replaced in commodity and money fetishism are human relations and social values, such as rationality and fairness, or social justice. It is these relations and values that are the real things. So if not oil and money, what kind of social relations should we associate with distributive social justice?

Any view of a social system without action aimed at its change and amelioration immediately uncovers its inertness, unfairness, and inhumanity. Any view of such a social order is likely to be a false one, an ideological charade created and maintained for the benefit of certain real interests. Such conservative social order cannot be successful for a long historic time as it holds back unstoppable social development. Only a developing social order is stable, one where institutional norms are continuously adapted to requirements of ongoing social actions aimed at their change. On the other hand, and no less paradoxically, a progressive social action can only be successful if it conforms to norms of prevailing institutional order. Many revolutions are crushed, and rebels are jailed or hanged simply because they violate generally accepted norms of institutional social order. How is it then that some social movements do succeed?

Social action always goes against some rules of the system. To be successful it should not violate the rest of them, it must conform to them. Civil rights and women's movements were successful because they were not total but rather particular group- and issue-oriented. This leads us to a conclusion that the thin and abstract notion of the relationship between action and social practices must be made more concrete as well as differentiated. Instead of the extreme and therefore abstract analytical levels of individuals and society we should move to the intermediate level of social groups, especially stratified ones. Today's social reality is better understood in terms of class practices of status group action. Any step in this direction requires that the concepts of class and status be at the center of any social analysis. The relationships among status groups and classes can be best understood in terms of values and standards of rationality and fairness that move them.

The knowledge of processes going on at the macro-social and micro-social levels provides a necessary background for deepening our knowledge of the meso-level relationships between status groups and shared class interests, but in itself it is always deficient. The macro-social structures that shape our civilization are outcomes of major social movements responsible for Western democracy and the Industrial revolution. They are finished social products so to speak. Their research inevitably retreats into the infinite questions of world history and global society. The study of individual consciousness is also bound to retreat into the infinite depths of the human mind and its reflexivity. Only limited by the practical urgency and concreteness of achieving social justice and progressive social development can these important studies acquire their proper place and meaningful anchorage.

Social Circulation

Social exchange and distribution are fundamental to economic science. Keynes advocated spending and consumption rather than saving to achieve higher employment. However, this policy can be effective and helpful only in kicking off economic recovery such as after the Great Depression. With WWII intervening, the causes of the Great Depression were not revealed, and its lessons were not learned. Behind Keynes' ideas there was the vision of economic circulation and exchange between businesses and households. According to that vision, businesses supply consumer goods and services to households in exchange for resources (factors of production) that are received from households. Households create consumer expenditures with the help of income that they receive from businesses. The two opposite flows of this exchange are said to reconcile in the money market. We can propose an alternative view of social exchange, exchange in human terms, one between status groups and classes. In this alternative conception, goods, services, income and resources will appear as indicators of the two opposite flows between status groups and classes, similarly both substantive and symbolic.

Exchange is indeed a fundamental form of social relations. Yet economic science masks these social relations by focusing on their reified aspects. By contrast, sociology can focus on exchange relations among and within stratified status groups and social classes. Instead of businesses we will speak of social structures of upper, lower and middle classes. The structures of social classes provide status groups with their achievement, their practices, their satisfaction, and their aspirations. In return, the structures of status groups supply classes with values without which the latter could not operate. These are the symbolic values of fairness, appropriateness,[3] enjoyment,[4] and trust. The opposite flow consists in status groups generating class interest, class confidence, class action, and class structure. In return, class structures provide status groups with their values of equity, of instrumental and value reason, and of hope.[5] The two flows of exchange are reconciled by standards of status and class consistency.

Thus the relations within and among social classes are responsible, in the final analysis, for the structures of social status groups such as family, educational, or occupational ones just as the relations within and among status groups are responsible for class structures such as settlement, industry, and financial. In the final analysis, all historic social change can be seen as mutual adjustments between achieved status and class, between social practices and class action, between status satisfaction and class confidence, or between status aspiration and class interest. Similarly on the value side there are constant mutual adjustments going on between our ideals of equity and those of fairness, of rationality and reason, of trust and belief.

Status practices and status satisfaction mediate between status achievement and status aspirations. In a similar way, class action and class confidence mediate between class structure and class interest. What we have here is a mutual interdependence of conscious and habitual, of personal and impersonal, of voluntaristic and institutional. The key to evaluating all these exchanges is in comparisons of their unique modes, the only facet that can be present them in commensurable forms. Prevailing modes of social distribution and exchange may all have historic origins, but as Lenin discovered in the 1920's, and as Chinese communists are discovering it today, they all survive and continue to operate in present social relations. What makes a difference is the weight of particular modes in their structural settings. Modes of social distribution concern allocation of achieved social status and class. Modes of social exchange are relevant to status practices and class action. It is in terms of these modes that we can fruitfully analyze the value of fairness that is central to standards of social distribution and exchange.

The relationship between the ideal of distributive justice and prevailing unfair social structures can be described as polar opposites mediated by the mechanism of social exchange and orientations to it where the two opposites interpenetrate. Associating social distribution and exchange whether of status or class relations with established areas of sociological study may be not so straightforward. Social exchange has been seen as the foundation of every human interaction since Homans' early studies. We can speak of both status group practices and class action in terms of social exchange. Status group practices are guided by orientations, generally in the form of public opinion that can be evaluated for its rationality. This can be further specified as either satisfaction-dissatisfaction with achieved (or inherited) social status.

Describing status group practices in terms of exchange is not problematic conceptually, but can orientations to status group practices be translated into relations of fair social distribution or allocation? This will make sense only if public opinion is conceived as an artifact formed for stratified status group as well as for class structures. If we can show that social life revolves around modes of distribution and exchange between social status group aspirations and their shared class interests; and that these relations can be measured and presented as the first social reality, then we may be able to demonstrate that perhaps not all that is solid melts into air, and that social science makes good sense and has its practical uses.

Notes

[1] Zukin and DiMaggio (1990); Swedberg (1991); Smelser and Swedberg (1994); Zafirovski (1999, 2001, 2006).

[2] Baudrillard (1981); Chikszentmihalyi and Rochberg-Halton (1981).

[3] For value in status practices this seems better than Weber's "habitual orientation."

[4] Weber articulated this value of status satisfaction as "affectual orientation."

[5] These values are what Parsons was searching as "symbolic media of societal interchange" analogous to money.

2

The Sociological Method

Social theories become increasingly obsolete and irrelevant with the passage of time. That includes the works of sociological classics. Yet we keep using their conceptual language, the only common professional language learned by every new generation of sociologists. This is how students acquire concepts of the working class, of bureaucracy and ideal types, of organic solidarity, and of the social system. And this is what becomes objective social reality for them. There can be no firmly established truths in social sciences, only certain generalizations valid for limited periods of time and for local conditions. Spencer's laws of growth and of structural or functional differentiation are hardly remembered by sociologists today, nor are Marx's laws of the falling rate of profit and of the impoverishment of the working class. What, then, do we value in the sociological classics? If it is not their substantive theories, then it must be the methods they used in producing those theories as well as their central concepts.

Having to do with the overall process of developing new social-scientific knowledge rather than with its products, these methods form the bedrock on which substantive social theories and conceptual schemes rest. In this sense, sociology as a whole can be seen as a scientific method - as Durkheim and Simmel did. It was in this broad sense of the word that they spoke of sociology as a distinct social science characterized by its own method. The method of sociological deconstruction and reconstruction represents all phases of social science thought processes – from the de-objectifying understanding of classic authorities to their re-objectifying conceptualization, and from de-subjectifying interpretation to re-subjectifying explanation. A special method is also developed to measure social structures and their mutual consistency. Deviations of empirical social structures from these standards will be treated as (positive or negative, tolerable or excessive) deviations from the values used as standards in social distribution and exchange.

The Quest for Reality

Let us recall C. Wright Mills' critique of the disconnect between what he called Grand Theory and Abstract Empiricism. These two notions remain by and large applicable to sociology today. To do justice to Parsons, it must be said that *The Social System* against which C. Wright Mills' critique of Grand Theory was directed had a strong hermeneutic foundation in *The Structure of Social Action.*[1] The notion of Grand Theory is more applicable to the classic authorities whose ideas Parsons reinterpreted and then reconceptualized in his subsequent works. It can be applied to Parsons' work only if we use it for our own reconceptualization. The same can be said of Marx even though his voluminous *Theories of Surplus-Value* was written after *The Capital.* But when today we take Marx, Weber, Durkheim, and Parsons as classic authorities, when we recognize them all as the undisputed foundation for our sociological work and use their works as material for our own hermeneutic reinterpretation and reconceptualization, then they can all be legitimately called Grand Theories. So how do we see social reality today? How has its vision changed, especially over the last century and a half?

According to Mannheim, all ideologies are forms of false consciousness when adopted separately and uncritically – unless they are consistently fused together in a *verstehende* reinterpretation and reconceptualization oriented to empirical research relevant to contemporary social concerns. Grand Theories become utopias when rather than using them as material for de-objectifying understanding and de-subjectifying interpretation they are treated as describing objective reality and when attempts are made to build or promote social movements aimed at institutionalizing such utopias. "Real utopias," especially the extreme ones of either left or right, substitute ready-made ideology for the laborious but necessary methods of social sciences. They can be dangerous. As the history of the 20th century shows, in times of crisis utopias can and have been made real by seductive demagogical leaders putting them into practice by force.

The falsehoods of ideology and utopia can be avoided in what Mannheim called a quest for reality.[2] As political reality can only be found in a synthesis of conflicting partisan positions, so must sociology synthesize its particular ideological conceptions that must, in turn, be subjected to new, revised syntheses as time goes on. "The continuously revised and renewed synthesis of the existing particular viewpoints becomes all the more possible because the attempts at synthesis have no less a tradition than has the knowledge founded on partisanship," wrote Mannheim.[3] By synthesizing Grand Theories in (continuously revised) conceptual frameworks we can create two mediating forms of this social science where they interpenetrate: hermeneutic reinterpretation of classic legacies and causal explanation where multiple alternative theories can be constructed and tested. True sociological consciousness can find reality only in critical amalgamations of classic conceptual legacies. Their reconceptualization and reinterpretation that has preoccupied much of sociological work does not have to take several volumes or even one thick volume. It can be done in a few short chapters. Construction and testing of substantive social theories is better seen as part of research work quite separate from conceptual and interpretive work.

There are two main ways suggested for reading sociological classics. One is the presentist way of interpreting them with a view of applying their ideas to today's social relations that are different from those that the classic authors themselves had in mind.[4] The other way is historicist, the opposite way in a sense, that mandates the reading of classics in their own context and without adding any interpretive language at all that was not used by the classics themselves.[5] There is also a phenomenological way suggested for reading the meanings of historic texts as lived ones, unmediated symbolically by speech. According to Rock,[6] this gives us "an opportunity to enter into the forms and content of life prepared by the dead. The seizing of such an opportunity becomes a phenomenological reality grounded in the present." This method can be seen as a special, extreme case of historicism.

A fourth way of reading the classics is their deconstruction that is supposed to combine and supersede the extremes of both the objectivism of the historicist way and the constructivism of the presentist one.[7] Indeed, both the historicist and the presentist methods are valuable in their own right only if used jointly and sequentially. To interpret classical works with a view to today's tasks in sociology, we must first understand their original historic meanings. Without such an understanding any interpretation can easily slip into a distorted, arbitrary picture of the classics. And without interpretation, a historicist reading alone remains just an academic exercise devoid of practical usefulness outside the academy. As interpretation needs understanding, so must understanding be followed by interpretation. There is no middle ground between interpretation and understanding. The term interpretive understanding is a poor translation of Weber's *Verstehen*.

An initial historicist reading of a classic would explore his main themes and in so doing reveal his key concepts and categories. This would make it possible to evaluate how well substantive classic themes were worked out with the help of those concepts and categories. In a subsequent interpretation we would use classic concepts and categories revealed in prior reading with a view of developing our own themes relevant to today's sociological concerns. So first we read the classics in a purely historicist mode striving at understanding them in their own terms. The new element here may be in the selection of themes and in the emphasis laid on some of them as against others. Such choices will usually prefer seminal, original elements of classical works. As Jones said,[8] we always decide "what is worthy of study." Also, certain relationships among selected themes may be brought to light. Thus, in reading Weber, for example, we will want to show a thematic unity across his major works - *Protestant Ethic*, *Economy and Society*, and his sociology of religion. We will want to elucidate his central substantive and methodological categories, such as ideal types of legitimate domination, of orientation of social action; his methodology of historic causation. We may want to pay special attention to Weber's idea of value-rationality as a property of social action or of action orientation, and to the theme of value-freedom as Weber's normative take on the relationship between theory and practice. A similar approach will be useful in reading Marx, Durkheim, and Parsons.

After completing the historicist reading, we will interpret classic ideas and concepts with a view of addressing today's problems in social science and in sociological practice. We will now want to re-interpret their previously understood meanings, and in this way de-subjectify them. This is where we switch to a presentist perspective. We interpret classic concepts and categories in the light of today's sociological concerns. Since the number of interpretations of the same texts is limitless, the criteria for evaluating interpretations must be the completeness of the material covered and the internal consistency of the interpretation itself. Different interpretations of the classics do not necessarily negate each other - if for no other reason than because the classical texts themselves show changes of position and are not free of ambiguities and contradictions. Preference may depend on readers' interpretive interests. We will also want to find valuable commonalities among them. In doing so we may feel free to change somewhat the exact meanings intended by the classics and to adapt their language to today's needs. This will become necessary especially if we then want to construct our own conceptual scheme rather than simply follow Weber as against Marx or Durkheim as against Parsons.

Again, the reading of the classics must be a narrative that is internally consistent with respect to a sociologist's perspective and with regard to the classic texts. It can consist of several layers not necessarily separated in time and in space. So first comes a historicist reading in Jones' sense – a reading covering possibly most of the classic legacies without, however, losing their internal unity. Here we elucidate the classics' seminal concepts and categories of thought – both substantive and methodological. One can also address certain unresolved problems found in the classic legacy, such as the relationship between theory and practice in Marx, the problem of positive functions of crime in Durkheim or the problem of value-neutrality in Weber. In such a re-reading, we should find that central classic sociological concepts - exploitation and class struggle, social values and rationalization, solidarity and social coordination, social integration and exchange - were all rooted substantively or reflexively, for example, in problems of social justice and sustainable social development as the most fundamental issues of today's social order. This first stage is purely historicist. Having done that, we use our gained understanding of the classics to de-subjectifying their ideas and the senses intended in their conceptual schemes and categories by re-interpreting them.

In a subsequent re-subjectifying conceptualization we extract the classic concepts and categories out of their historical contexts and use them as material in building our own conceptual schemes still making an effort to do as little violence to their original meanings as possible. We reframe classic sociological legacies by combining and re-combining some of their central ideas and categories in an internally consistent conceptual scheme of our own. This must involve above all the concepts of social class, of status group, and of the relationship between them. We can also compare and integrate Marx's and Weber's historicism, then Durkheim's and Parsons' functionalism, and then see how the classic historicist and functionalist ideas could be fused together in a working concept of progressive social development. It is also useful at this stage critically to find inconsistencies or unresolved problems in the classic texts. That could involve either problems of the classics' professed methodologies or their substantive themes or possibly inconsistencies between the two.

Sociological Deconstruction and Reconstruction

Neither hermeneutic understanding nor interpretation is an end in itself. Their primary task is to provide necessary material foundation for a consistent re-conceptualization of conflicting extant usages so that such a re-conceptualization may be grounded and have a chance of being considered valid - if only for a limited time. At this third stage of conceptualization we consistently combine certain ideas and concepts of all the four sociological classics in a single synthesizing conception. This was done by Marx himself with respect to classical English economists and French socialists, and by Parsons with respect to Marshall, Pareto, Durkheim, and Weber. In this way we may hope to use our understanding of the classics to articulate a better concept of and a research method for solutions to today's social problems such as social justice and sustainable social order. We will not be concerned with literally following the meanings of the categories used in the original works of Marx, Weber, Durkheim or Parsons. While still trying to preserve as much of their original meaning as possible, we may nevertheless take them out of their original context and adapt them to the problems of today's social concerns. In this way, we can re-conceptualize the ideas of the sociological classics as if they all saw different aspects of one and the same ideal object.[9]

But is there such a single perspective that will be congruent with the conceptual and methodological legacy of all the four sociological classics who were so different after all? The answer must be yes since according to a general consensus existing in sociology, they are all relevant to our today's efforts in building a valid and useful social science. So the question should rather be how do we find – or construct – such a single perspective? This is equivalent to asking, what relevance does the work of the classical sociologists have for us today? Which classical concepts and methods are meaningful in today's social realities? There is also a requirement that combining the classics' central concepts should not be eclectic. The new conceptual scheme must be internally coherent and consistent. All this means that after de-objectifying the classics in the process of their understanding, the work of de-subjectifying interpretation must be based on a synthesizing conceptualization that re-objectifies classic ideas and concepts in a new internally coherent scheme.

Having interpreted classic legacies and used these interpretations to build our new conceptual schemes we can re-objectify classic ideas, concepts and categories by using them in causal explanation, in theory construction and in subsequent empirical testing. This will involve modeling the objects of empirical investigations and thus creating a basis for quantitative empirical research of present-day problems such as social justice. This creates a basis for constructing a variety of substantive social theories and for their empirical testing that includes modeling and measurement. Quantitatively modeled and measured social structures, social practices, and their underlying social values will make it possible to evaluate past and present social processes and prepare for the future.[10] We can do all that because our de-objectifying understanding and re-objectifying explanation are mediated by de-subjectifying interpretation and re-subjectifying conceptualization.

This symmetric picture is complicated by the fact that while any understanding and interpretation needs an ontological frame of reference, in a sense this relationship holds the other way, too. Any ontological presupposition can only be expressed in, justified by, and based upon an understanding and interpretation of their meanings that are substantive and concrete in some other, extraneous context. This is what has been described as the hermeneutic circle of understanding. Such a circle can be broken and avoided when the task of semantic understanding and interpretation proper is separated from the reflexive critique of prevailing misunderstandings and misinterpretations as well as from the critical analysis of pertinent literary material. In a similar structural process Saussure insisted on separating observed collective phenomena of human speech (*langage*) and individual acts of communication (*parole*) from language proper (*langue*) as consisting of evaluated syntagmatic and associative relations of meaningful signs.

The idea of a hermeneutic circle harks back to Hegel's dictum that what is rational is real (is actualized in the historic development of human Spirit), and what is real is rational. The latter is not necessarily true, however. At any present moment we are faced with multiple realities whose rationality must be questioned. Ontological presuppositions that are always present in our interpretive work are also likely to be polysemantic. Attempts at their explicit interpretation will immediately expose their biases that cannot be rationally justified. Gadamer appropriately called such presuppositions prejudices. But this is just another way of saying that interpretation is an outcome of mediation between understanding and explanation with an emphasis on understanding. Conceptualization is also a mediating product standing between de-objectifying understanding and re-objectifying explanation. The difference is in emphasis on explanation – explanation of the core realities contained in classic sociology such as social injustice and irrationality that are as germane to today's social realities as ever.

As with any other value, rationality judgments presume certain normative standards, and such standards are not unproblematic. Philosophers, ever since Hume, have debated the question of whether it is possible to derive "ought" from "is," and they have answered it in the negative. This is because in the process of the debate, the distinction between "is" and "ought" was replaced with one between facts and values. However, while "is" indeed refers to facts, "ought" refers to prescriptions of conduct or of public policy that are always based on evaluations of facts rather than on values themselves. In the context of social science "ought" can be conceived as a reversal of evaluated facts' deviations – especially of excessive ones – from standards of social values such as social justice.

Unlike preliterate societies, Western civilization preserves its history as accumulated developmental experience, and uses it to learn from successes and failures of the past. The heart of the problem is not in the values themselves, whether high or mundane, but in the standards we use in evaluating the past and the present. No one-dimensional record of social development can provide standards of social values however, since it is always involved with one partisan interest or another. The classics of sociology saw standards of social justice and rationality in the historic interplay of stratified meso-social realities. They explained conflicts between status groups and classes, their rise and fall by structural inconsistencies between them. And they endeavored to reconstruct this two-dimensional view of social development in their efforts to learn from the past and help build a better future.

The promise given by neatly built conceptual schemes successfully to grasp and interpret empirical social reality never comes without a price. Genuine lived meanings of empirical data are always fuzzy, haphazard, and ultimately unfathomable. While the harmony, comprehensiveness, and consistency imposed by an extraneous conceptual scheme on observed lived meanings may obviate the problem of reliability, the extreme rationality of abstract conceptual meanings may easily rob them of their original validity. Common-sense native meanings cannot be simply replaced with sociological conceptual jargon. The precipice separating them can only be bridged by meanings that are intelligible both in terms of deductively obtained abstract conceptual schemes and in terms of the unique meanings that constitute the language of a local community of natives.

If we have a comprehensive system of such meanings, we can then leap into the less tidy but necessary realm of empirical research. There we will have to readjust our vision to the new perspective. From abstract ideas and concepts such as social process and social structure we will have to come down to the real world of sociological observation and measurement. Reports of indices of social justice could provide quantitative estimates of the levels of justice and injustice in our society with respect to particular facets of its social structures. We can then estimate quantitatively to what degree the social structures of our interest are fair or unfair.

C. Wright Mills' critique of Abstract Empiricism was directed against social research where atomized individuals rather than status groups and classes pursuing their interests were taken as units of analysis, and substantive conclusions were often inductively drawn from spurious relationships among variables found with the help of poorly specified mathematical models. Social research of this kind is not unheard of in today's sociology either.[11] In building our concepts and quantitative models of social justice we will seek to combine their aspects found in the sociological classics and to integrate prevailing ideological modes of social distribution and exchange. We will distinguish between the ideas of status groups and social classes that are still routinely used as interchangeable in American sociological literature. Following Marx, Weber and Sorokin, we will show that they stand for two different if interrelated, orthogonal realms of social relations. It can then be shown that status group and class structures, and their corresponding symbolic values can be successfully modeled in sociology, and that standards of rationality and fairness can be effectively used to evaluate current social trends. We can show how empirical social research can help attain better social justice by aligning modes of social distribution and exchange.

Notes

[1] Parsons' conceptual synthesis of the classic legacies of his time was not, however, brought to the concluding stage of re-objectifying modeling and measurement. The same is true of the sociological deconstructions produced by Habermas and Alexander.

[2] "The attempt to escape ideological and utopian distortions is, in the last analysis, a quest for reality. […] All the conflicting groups and classes in society seek this reality in their thought and deeds, and it is therefore no wonder that it appears to be different to each of them. […] The special cultural sciences from the point of view of their particularity are no better than everyday empirical knowledge" (Mannheim, 1985, pp. 98, 101-102).

[3] Mannheim (1985, p. 151).

[4] Seidman (1985).

[5] Jones (1977).

[6] Rock (1976, p. 363).

[7] Kelly (1990).

[8] Jones (1977, p. 284).

[9] See Schedrovitsky (1971).

[10] As used here, the term reconstruction is intended in juxtaposition to preliminary hermeneutic deconstruction as its necessary methodological as well as terminological complement. It has nothing to do with Habermas' (1976, 1979) notion of "reconstructive science" that is thoroughly individualistic modeled as it is on Freud's psychoanalysis, Piaget's concept of child development, and Chomsky's concept of linguistic competence. To numerous critics of this idea Habermas responded by modifying or qualifying his claims and conclusions that were based, nevertheless, on the criticized original distinctions (see McCarthy, 1978; Árnason, 1982; Schmid, 1982; Alford, 1985).

[11] Lieberson (1985), Lieberson and Lynn (2002).

3

Historic Change in Modes of Production

Karl Marx was a prolific and profound writer. His works burst with philosophical and literary knowledge and wit as well as a deep understanding of the intellectual problems of his time. If there was a subject-matter he did not master, his studies not only quickly gave him the missing knowledge, but also produced results that were on the cutting edge of that field. This was the case with literary theory, mathematics, and political economy. *Capital*, Marx's crowning achievement, is still read today despite the demise of communist political regimes. While Marx's empirical social reality is gradually becoming irrelevant, we still consider him a founding father of sociology. Marx introduced concepts that have become part of our common stock of knowledge as well as language. Some of the problems he raised are still with sociology as a discipline. Marx was also an angry rebel determined to change the course of human history. The meaning of his entire intellectual legacy generated heated debates. His intellectual and political achievements remain as controversial today as they were in his lifetime.

In Marx's epistemology, being and economic, property relations were primary. Consciousness, political institutions and ideas, philosophy and theory in general were secondary. They were but expressions of the self-serving ideology of the capitalist class. The inevitable progression of socio-economic formations and the coming of communism was the fundamental law of history and the only true foundation for a valid social theory. And yet, the class struggle on which the actual coming of the next formation depended was not climaxing in a proletarian revolution. The proletarian revolution was supposed to be in political praxis, in the usurpation of political power in Europe without which the nationalization of private property of means of production was not possible. To stage a revolution, the working class had to be united and inspired. To achieve that, it needed a universally valid, philosophically and methodologically founded, strictly scientific, radically new interpretation of the capitalist mode of production. To be radical such a theory had to assume the perspective of the proletariat as the class standing for universal public interest. This was the circle of the theory-and-practice problem which Marx faced in his London exile. How did he resolve it?

Class Struggle in History

Marx saw historic social development as successive changes of socio-economic formations. He associated the three big periods of Western history - Antiquity, Middle Ages, and Modernity – with slavery, feudalism and capitalism understood as modes of social production. The changes of these formations were explained by historic discrepancies between the immanent development of technology and industry as productive forces, on the one hand, and corresponding – yet usually lagging - forms of relations of production reflecting conflicts between antagonistic classes, on the other. The two major classes of Marx's time - workers and capitalists – were seen as outcomes of unequal historic processes of capital accumulation, originally through trade and land expropriation, where capital was defined as private property. Extrapolating this view of past history seen as a social-scientific law, Marx concluded that the demise of capitalism as a particular historic mode of production was inevitable. He saw the industrial working class as the primary motive force in bringing about this demise, and the future communist society as one where means of production would be nationalized eliminating classes altogether.[1]

Marx arrived at this conclusion via Hegel and Feuerbach. Following Feuerbach's general materialistic critique of Hegel's philosophy and using Feuerbach's method of logical conversion, Marx expressed a strong disagreement with the substantive content of Hegel's social philosophy. Hegel was concerned (in his *Philosophy of Right*) with the problem of supersession, or harmonization of the particular interests of free individuals pursuing their goals as members of civil society and the universal interests of the state - the crown, the executive power, etc. – as an external necessity imposing on the freedom of individuals. Hegel saw civil servants, the greater part of the middle class, as the universal class able to give an adequate representation in the legislature, and thus in the executive, to the multitude of the particular interests of all members of civil society. He asserted that this particular land-owning middle class was perfectly capable of adapting itself to such a role: its moral life was concentrated on the family, the most stable of all social institutions, its inalienable right of private property assured an independent source of livelihood and thus, stability and incorruptibility in the uncertainties of otherwise changing profits on capital investments, as well as independence from the influences of changing political winds.[2]

Feuerbach was the first to suggest the importance of a critique of Hegel's *Philosophy of Right* for the destruction of his entire system. He proposed to "turn the predicate into the subject" From this followed the principle, "The true relationship of thought to being is only this: being is the subject, thought the predicate."[3] Following Feuerbach's lead, Marx presented Hegel's doctrine of civil society and the state as human social reality seen from the perspective of logic only illustrated with elements of the political theories of his time. As the young Marx wrote, "Hegel's true interest is not the philosophy of right, but logic. The task of philosophy is not to understand how thought can be embodied in political determinations but to dissolve the existing political determinations into abstract ideas. The concern of philosophy is not the logic of the subject-matter but the subject-matter of logic. Logic does not provide a proof of the state but state provides the proof of logic."[4]

In accordance with that principle, the goal of the working-class movement could be achieved by a second mediation of two immediate opposites - the unique opposite expressed in the principle of alienated labor and private property, and communism as the universal opposite. The first mediation was a critical analysis of prevailing particular conditions of the working class. The second mediation of the same two opposites was a positive reflexive formulation of the particular principles of ethical life – the historic praxis of working-class movement. This second mediation was a reflexive one in that it relied on the results of the above primary mediation. It led in the opposite direction, from the second member of the initial abstract juxtaposition, i.e., from the previously formulated universal opposite of communism, to the first, unique one: capitalism. The two complementary mediations in Marx' conception of a dialectical transition to communism mutually justified and reinforced each other. This dynamic of the critical-negative and constructive-positive mediation is also clearly seen in many smaller fragments of Marx' substantive dialectic, notably in his ideas of labor and commodity production as mediating between nature and man, and of capital as mediating between alienated labor and its products.

Thus, by simply transposing the subjects and predicates in the syllogisms underlying Hegel's statements, Marx reformulated the problem declaring the (particular) interests of the proletariat as universal - rather then those of Hegel's propertied civil servants. This led Marx to the conclusion that the proletariat was the only class capable of accomplishing the historical mission of transcending the inhuman consequences of alienation from the enormous productive forces developed in Europe by that time. Based on that materialistic premise, Marx dismissed prevailing forms of public consciousness, whether political, legal, or philosophical, as forms of self-serving bourgeois ideology. The main content of Marx's *Capital* can be described as its subtitle, "A Critique of Political Economy," mainly in this implicit sense, as a systematic description of the inhumanity and immorality of the capitalist social order aimed at awakening the working class consciousness, i.e., as the first alternative to bourgeois political economy posed by Engels' "Outlines."

According to Engels, capitalist economy is always reproduced in a disproportionate manner so that either the means of production are underemployed for lack of sufficient labor-power, or the workers are underemployed for lack of corresponding production capacities, or else the stock of products grows without finding sufficient demand. This capitalist "anarchy of production" always carries in itself the possibility of economic crises.[5] Capitalist production also inevitably consolidates the working class. The united industrial workers are prepared for class struggle by their sheer numbers, but above all, by the inevitable realization of the striking inequities created by capitalist social exchange. On top of all that, the anarchy of capitalist reproduction, of exchange relations creates the general conditions for economic breakdown through recurrent crises. Capitalist production "begets, with the inexorability of a natural process, its own negation." It establishes "individual property on the basis of the achievements of the capitalist era; namely co-operation and the possession in common of the land and the means of production produced by labor itself."[6]

Therefore, Engels wrote, political economy was deceiving itself about the realities of economic life and, by the same token, was serving the interest of property owners who were in a better position to exploit the discrepancy between theory and real life to their advantage than was the working class. In reality, under the domination of private property, supply did not follow demand, commodities were not sold at value, competition did not stimulate production, and so on. In reality, the economy was chronically fluctuating between production booms and slumps, and nothing at all could ever be said with certainty about the next development. The only law which applied to real economic life was "the law of the stronger." In accordance with that "law," large capital and large landed property swallowed small capital and small landed property with the middle classes disappearing "until the world is divided into millionaires and paupers." The choice political economy faced was between telling the ugly truth about the inhuman and immoral economic relations prevailing in society, or else changing the very premise of political economy by abolishing the rule of private property and thus altering the meaning of economic categories.

This critique of economic conditions had in its turn been prepared by Marx's preceding concern with the nature of contemporary political life as centered on the issue of the separation, or alienation, of man's life as a citizen from his communal life as a "true species-being" - the main thrust of Marx's reappraisal of Hegel's philosophy of right.[7] Instead of communal participation in political life as an end in itself, as an expression of human nature, Marx observed, man was reduced in bourgeois, or civil society, to an atomized and selfish, self-sufficient monad engaged in a never-ending Hobbesian war of all against all, including religious hostility, while the state served only as a means for safeguarding the individual freedoms of waging such a war, of pillaging, and of protecting the loot in the form of private property. Marx voiced similar harsh criticism of prevailing family relations and education, but his main attention was drawn to the critique of capitalist economy as the domain of human relations which, he believed, held the key to understanding all modern social institutions and where lay the roots of the polarization between the propertied capitalist class and the poor working class, or the proletariat.

But Marx did not stop at endorsing Feuerbach's reversal of Hegel's idealistic principle of the primacy of consciousness over being. Marx also adopted Hegel's historicism. Instead of Hegel's identity between the logical and the historical, Marx obtained the principle of identity between the historical - understood realistically rather than as knowledge - and the logical. It was this philosophical principle that underlay Marx' and Engels' conception of the revolutionary change of historic modes of production by class struggle and of the revolutionary dictatorship of the proletariat. Marx also rejected the idea that such transcending was a matter of proper representation in the legislature, and that the state, the corporation, and the family were essential, or necessary at all for the new communist form of society. It was in this sense that Marx began to speak of scientific communism. He proclaimed that scientific communism had nothing to do with crude or utopian socialism advocated by various European writers of his time.

Dialectic and Sustainable Social Development

Utopian socialism was concerned with pre-conceived specific forms of human communities or their social institutions while accepting the reality of private property and human self-alienation. Such conceptions, Marx argued, were foreign to genuine communism that was a product of totally new conceptual thinking presupposing the mediating transcendence - "the second supersession," or "the negation of negation" - of private property, and the ensuing uncompromising critique of prevailing political and economic practice.[8] The two opposites were mediated by a critique of the prevailing political economy, beginning with his "Excerpts From James Mill's Elements of Political Economy" through "Wage Labor and Capital," and followed by the presentation of Marx's own theory of political economy, initially in the *Grundrisse*, and then in *Capital*. The second mediation was in Marx's promotion of the working-class movement as praxis.

When Marx first characterized his method as ascension from the abstract to the concrete, he referred only to the *Grundrisse*[9] that he had just completed. In *Capital* this method was characterized as dialectical, and its distinctive feature was said to be an identification of the simplest abstraction comparable to the

cell in biology. The abstraction was to be made concrete in a series of oppositions to, and mediations of, other abstractions of
political economy. Indeed, Marx's full method can be seen as a
specification process of the abstract concept of commodity into
the more concrete concepts of price, wage, profit, land rent, and
interest.[10]

The relations of the four forms of value contained in
every commodity[11] were then transferred to the four phases in
the capitalist economy and to the four social classes that were
identified with them. Property owners are to the working class as
use-value is to abstract value-form; they stand in opposition to
each other as singular to universal. Industrial capitalists and merchants are the two social classes corresponding to exchange-value
and general monetary value-form which is another expression of
the particular mediating between the singular and the universal.
Despite the capitalists' mediating role, Marx presented them as
standing in a direct opposition to the working class.[12]

Marx saw consumption, production, exchange, and distribution as coterminous with use-value, universal abstract value,
exchange-value, and general value-form, or money. Both sets of
relations were identical with the relations in a regular syllogism.
Since consumption is both the last moment of the four and also
"[reacting] in turn upon the point of departure and [initiating] the
whole process anew,"[13] one can say that the movement of economic activity passes from singular (individual) consumption having to do with use-values to universal (social) production involving the abstract values of labor-power via the particular (industry-
wide, national) exchange of exchange-values and the distribution
of general monetary value-forms. The rest of *Capital* is then a detailed critical reinterpretation of these economic functional
phases as exploitation of the working class by capitalists with the
assistance of merchants and bankers.

While exploitation in consumption was related to workers' employment in industry, and exploitation in exchange was
seen as facilitated by the merchant class as aiders and abettors of
the capitalists, exploitation in production was associated with the

idea of surplus-value. For the process of capitalist production to begin, the capitalist must purchase human labor-power as a means of production. The value of labor-power is measured, like that of any other commodity, by the amount of the labor-power socially necessary for its manufacture. Thus, it becomes equivalent to the value of the means of subsistence necessary for the maintenance and procreation of its carrier, the proletariat. The capitalist agrees to remunerate the workers he employs only to that extent - but not before their labor-power is exercised, e.g., at the end of the working week. Worker's wages, on the other hand, can only buy the means of individual consumption necessary to regenerate and to perpetuate his labor-power. Consequently, from the cynical perspective of bourgeois society, the "maintenance and reproduction of the working class [as a whole is] a necessary condition for the reproduction of capital." Surplus-value is the increment obtained in commodity production over invested capital. The rate of surplus-value is measured by its ratio to variable capital, the part of advanced capital spent for the purchase of necessary labor-power that is expended and renovated in daily labor process. [14] The latter is the universal abstract value of a worker's labor-power, while the use-value of productive labor-power is labor itself activated by the capitalist after he hires the worker. Thus surplus-value is the value of labor-power in circulation, its exchange-value and its general value-form.

Capitalists increase the rate of surplus-value and the degree of exploitation in production by extending the working day to its natural 24-hours' limit which is called production of absolute surplus-value. The same effect is achieved by decreasing the value of labor-power and thus, the amount of necessary labor within the same length of the working day. The latter, called production of relative surplus-value, is achieved through higher labor productivity in those industries and those commodities "that contribute towards the necessary means of subsistence, and are therefore elements of the value of labor-power." Higher labor productivity is achieved through technological innovations and co-operation, or by intensifying labor, particularly by adjusting the tempo of living labor to that of machines.[15]

The critical reinterpretation of capitalist exploitation in social exchange breaks down into the questions of a worker's wage, entrepreneurial profit, banking interest, and commercial profit, as well as the ancillary question of rent. Except for wage considered in Volume One, the correspondence of these four categories of class exchange to those of value is not made explicit by Marx. At the very least, however, their foursome division must be seen as significant. Had Marx applied the same deductive logic to the categories of exchange, he could have similarly argued that industrial profit, wage, commercial profit, and interest also relate to one another as (second-order) use-value, universal abstract value, exchange-value and general value-form. Indeed, this argument could have been put to a good use to forestall the controversies that have arisen around Volume Three since it was published, notably the so-called transformation problem of Chapter 9. Besides the more obvious feedback relation between exchange circulation and (re)distribution, something that can account for any direction in the change of locally and historically concrete rates of profit as well as other exchange categories, the seeming paradoxes of capitalist exchange may arise from the dual range of values involved in exchange: prices, or surplus-values in their ultimate form of money as a general equivalent, and the same surplus-values in the form of money as a special commodity in its own right, e.g., as gold. Only in banking interest does money appear in its special-commodity form, while in entrepreneurial profit, wage, and commercial profit it can be in either of its two forms, more exactly, it is always in both forms simultaneously.

Such is the deductive movement of Marx's thought in *Capital* in terms of the elementary structure of commodity as the embodiment of the four types of economic value. Marx's ascent from the abstract to the concrete in *Capital* did not strictly follow that order. In Volume One subtitled "The Process of Production of Capital," Marx primarily discussed unequal exchange between workers' means of subsistence and their labor-power spent in production. In the same Volume One, Marx also began the discussion of simple and extended reproduction, another issue in exchange, as well as of wages which was an issue in distribution. Apparently, he decided to digress from his method and give the readers a taste of his entire project in political economy already in Volume One, the only volume he lived to prepare for publication himself. In Volume Three, subtitled "The Process of Capitalist Production as a Whole," Marx intended to "present concrete forms which grew out of the process of capital's movement" and which would "approach step by step the form in which they appear on the surface of society."[16] But he actually continued a detailed analysis of distribution without justifying why it should now be treated as more concrete than exchange discussed in Volume Two.

Volume Two of *Capital* with its ideal reproduction schemes is the most puzzling of the three volumes. Dealing with criteria for establishing ideal proportions between investment and accumulation as well as consumption, these schemes are not supposed to be realized under capitalism. According to Marx, the non-observance of such ideal proportions under capitalism brought crises of overproduction, unemployment, and antagonistic class struggle. By implication, the realization of such proportions would establish a control of the social division of labor, something that he believed was possible only in a communist society. Reproduction schemes belonged rather to the political economy of communism, where capitalist anarchy of unfair market exchange would be corrected by centrally planned communist distribution. But with wage labor and capitalist profits ruled out in the system of direct communist distribution, and the market mechanism with its unpredictable spontaneous forces eliminated, contemplated redistributive justice could have no place under communism either!

In any event, in Volume Two, Marx formulated, despite his overall communist position, elements of a sociology of sustainable development. He was led to these paradoxical conclusions by the logic of his method. Yet this result of Marx's mature period accounts only for part of his entire project. The deductive ascension to the complex in *Capital* relied on Marx's earlier extensive studies of political economy beginning with "Excerpts from James Mill's Elements of Political Economy" and "Wage Labor and Capital" - where Marx first proposed surplus working time as the measure of exploitation of the working class by capitalists. That work was continued in *Grundrisse*, and it culminated in 1859 in the concept of surplus-value (in *A Contribution to the Critique of Political Economy*). In 1861-1863 Marx supplemented these investigations of political economy with a detailed critique of its categories in what is known today as *Theories of Surplus-Value*.[17] Thus Marx's overall project included both positive and critical movements of thought. The contradiction between his two epistemologies highlighted by Althusser[18] is resolved when we note that the basic principles of Marx's materialist conception of history were laid down already in his 1846 letter to Annenkov.[19]

As it becomes clear from his 1873 "Postface to the Second Edition" (of *Capital*, Volume One),[20] from his "Preface,"[21] and from the theses "Concerning Feuerbach,"[22] Marx also believed that he had transformed Hegel's idealist dialectic into his materialist kind. Two separate distinctions are involved here: materialism v. idealism and dialectic v. speculation. When engaging in a critique of his contemporary historical praxis, Marx indeed followed the materialist principle of beginning with the historically real, practical social world characterized by conflicts as well as by partisan ideologies. However, when accusing Feuerbach of (materialist) speculative thought and defending dialectic, Marx unlawfully separated what Hegel held as inseparable parts of a methodological whole.

In Hegel's *Logic,* dialectic had a negative-critical meaning. It referred to a critical movement of thought that follows understanding and precedes positive speculative reasoning. "In point of form Logical doctrine has three sides: (α) the Abstract side, or that of understanding; (ß) the Dialectical, or that of negative reason; (γ) the Speculative, or that of positive reason. [...] Thought, as Understanding, sticks to the fixity of characters and their distinctions from one another: every such limited abstract it treats as having subsistence and being of its own. [...] In the Dialectical stage these fine characterizations or formulae supersede themselves, and pass into their opposites. But when the Dialectical principle is employed by the understanding separately and independently [...] Dialectic becomes Skepticism; in which the result that ensues from its action is presented as a mere negation. [...] The Speculative stage, or stage of Positive reason, apprehends the unity of terms (propositions) in their opposition - the affirmative, which is involved in their disintegration and in their transition" [23]

Having adopted the principle of the primacy of being over consciousness and of praxis over theory, Marx reinterpreted Hegel's speculation as (abstract, idealist) antithesis of understanding, and critique as (materialist) synthesis. Historic praxis became for him a second necessary synthesis, a positive mediation between the interpenetrating polar opposites of speculation and understanding. The positive synthesis reversed the outcomes of negative critique. In accordance with this new method, Marx believed that the goal of the working-class movement – the *particular* historic praxis of abolishing exploitation - could be achieved by the mediation of two (interpenetrating) opposites - the *unique* critical analysis of prevailing conditions of the working class including alienated labor, on the one hand, and classless communist society as the *universal* opposite, on the other.

The epithet dialectical is justified as describing Marx's overall method only in the less specific sense of mediation, or supersession, that can be found within its fourth, positive-speculative moment as well. Although Engels may have been the first to use the term "dialectical materialism" in describing Marx's logic, he did not invent it by "extending historical materialism" as is believed by some commentators.[24] Despite the fact that Engels added, in his later works, a natural-philosophical interpretation to what was originally Marx's logical principle of a dialectical mediation between the opposites of primary, or material (and hence "materialist") being as the logical subject, and secondary, derived, or ideal (and hence "idealist") consciousness as the logical predicate, dialectical materialism in this sense was indeed the latent principle of the materialist conception of history.

Theory and Practice

In his early critical period, Marx saw praxis as an imperfect reality to be raised to the level of German philosophy which he considered to be the most advanced and, therefore, the universal theoretical consciousness of the time. Where Feuerbach only reversed the relationship between human consciousness and being as conceived by Hegel, as well as between philosophical theory and human practices, Marx declared that "the criticism of the speculative philosophy of law finds its progression not within itself but in tasks which can only be solved in one way - through practice. We must then ask ourselves: can Germany attain a practice *à la hauteur des principes*, that is to say, a revolution that raises it not only to the official level of modern nations but to the human level that will be their immediate future?" [25]

From that point on, Marx's purely philosophical concerns shifted to seeing that "theoretical needs be directly practical needs." The road to a revolutionary change in human practice passes through the wilderness of a similarly radical change in thought. Human practice changes drastically only to the extent theory is formulated in new concepts, i.e., with a radically new outlook on old theoretical problems. In its turn, theory "is capable of gripping the masses when it demonstrates ad hominem, and it demonstrates ad hominem as soon as it becomes radical. To be radical is to grasp things by the root." In this sense, revolutionary practice changes the circumstances of human social life while at the same time changing itself.[26]

In 1845-1850, Marx believed that a communist social revolution establishing a dictatorship of the proletariat was imminent in Germany and in the rest of Europe, and that it was practically around the corner. The revolutions did occur in 1848, but they were all suppressed. Marx initially described their defeat as little more than local and temporary failures of the predicted world communist revolution to materialize.[27] Somewhat later, he realized that the cause of achieving a radical social transformation was more complicated. It was time to go back to the drawing board, to a sober reappraisal of the situation, to theory. Existing theory was not perfect anymore. German idealist philosophy had been discarded as bourgeois ideology, but so was English political economy despite its materialist subject-matter. *Grundrisse* and *Capital* were the products of that mature concern.

Marx cooled down his revolutionary zeal in the British Museum where he began pondering on a fundamental universal-scientific reinterpretation of English political economy. He retained both ideas as his central conceptual scheme. The justification of this glaring inconsistency was in the universal-liberating role that Marx attributed to the proletariat as the motive force of the emerging communist mode of production. What was missing in this otherwise legitimate Hegelian phenomenology of spirit turned economic evolution was the proletarian revolution - the active factor. If only the working class could unite and establish its dictatorship, abolish the institutions of private property, the family, the State, and nationalize all means of production![28] The way to achieve such a revolution was to write a new perfect theory capable of gripping the masses and becoming a material force.

Having reduced all forms of social organization to their bare structural elements - classes - and all social phenomena to property tenure and labor, Marx narrowed his social science to the theme of workers' exploitation. This single-minded reduction was an attempt to reverse and correct his similar single-minded youthful passion for Romantic cosmic expansions. Before he converted to philosophical materialism, Marx was a devout idealist, an avid student of Hegel and German Romanticism in general, including that of Novalis, Schlegel, and Schelling, and going back to Fichte and Kant. In 1836-1837, during his first two years in Bonn as a student, and then in Berlin when Marx was already secretly engaged to Jenny von Westfalen, he wrote books of poetry to her.[29] In the true spirit of German Romanticism, the young Marx transformed his separation and frustrated love into problems of world and cosmic proportions. Hence the world-historical meanings of alienation in Marx's usage, of oneness through unity, and emancipation through dialectical supersession.[30]

Behind all of Marx's political economy and scientific communism, behind his historical materialism, and earlier humanistic communism, there lurked a deep and strong undercurrent of an ironic Romantic-idealist world-view that sought the salvation, or liberation of man in the resurrection of the long-gone Golden Age of mankind and in making that Golden Age a reality here and now or, at least, in the future. It was that "prehistoric age" of humanistic communism that Marx presented as the point of origin in the genesis of modern industry and commerce as well as of capitalist production relations. Engels later gave the name of "primitive Communistic society" to the same reality in his footnote to the 1888 English edition of the *Communist Manifesto*.[31] Marx never fully abandoned this Romantic primitive-communist line of thought. Traces of it can be found in *Grundrisse*,[32] in *A Contribution to the Critique of Political Economy*,[33] and in *Capital*.[34] The publication in 1877 of Lewis H. Morgan's *Ancient Society* only confirmed Marx's own thinking along similar lines. His notebooks on this subject[35] were used by Engels in writing *The Origin of the Family, Private Property, and the State*.[36]

Despite his ideological materialist reversal of the 1840's and a substitution of idealistic cosmic expansions with a similarly radical materialist-economic reductionism, Marx's youthful Romantic aspirations were preserved in his later work. His attempt to present the interests of the working class as universal was a highly ambivalent product of both of these extreme and antithetical movements of thought applied to the same reality simultaneously. While romantically universalizing the special interests and role of one social class, Marx was at the same time reducing the variety of its social interests to economic ones as prescribed by his equally absolutist materialist ideology. Marx never resolved this ambivalence, nor was he aware of it as far as can be seen.

Had he been able to resolve it, he would have seen that the retrospective evolutionary-developmental and the prospective activist-practical viewpoints need not be seen as mutually exclusive, but rather as justifying and supporting each other, and that, moreover, either of them could be applied to theory and practice simultaneously. Marx's concept of humanistic communism as a peculiar form of consciousness relevant to a specific historical reality was itself an "ideological superstructure" anchored in a certain "material social basis, or substructure." Such an application of the categories of Marx's historical materialism to his own early work would do justice both to the concept of humanistic communism and to the materialist conception of history. It would elucidate an essential element of Marx's overall thinking while verifying at the same time his general principle of historical materialism as a philosophy of history. He could have also rethought his concept of capitalist exploitation

Capitalist exploitation was an expression of the generally perceived reality that in the social exchange between non-working, only investing capitalists as a social class, and the class of working but materially non-investing proletarians, the proletariat came out as the loser. Marx interpreted the phenomenon of exploitation in terms of the labor theory of value - as capitalists' selfish and unfair appropriation of surplus-value - by contrasting the amount of labor power socially necessary for the production of commodities and its actual expenditure by workers beyond that necessity. Carried over from Adam Smith and Ricardo, this reduction was rejected by many classical economists, like Malthus and Say, even before it was left behind by the marginalist school. Those who are still struggling with the labor theory of value come to the conclusion that its reductionism implies the absurdity of exploitation of the dead and that it is simply irrelevant in interpreting exploitation.[37] More generally, Marx's professed conceptual scheme regarding labor as the only substantive source of all use-values and denying capital a similar productive role was inconsistent with the very notion of capitalism as a distinctive socio-economic formation.

Marx came up with the idea that surplus working time was the measure of workers' exploitation by capitalists in 1847 when he was unexpectedly invited to deliver a series of lectures before a workers' circle in Brussels. That was the time when a proletarian revolution was on everyone's mind in Germany and ten years before Marx began his serious work in political economy. Marx prepared those lectures in haste and later published them as "Wage Labor and Capital."[38] It was there that Marx suggested that, when viewed from the perspective of the working class, profit was determined not by the cost of production as "bourgeois economists" held it, but by the amount of labor time spent by workers in commodity production beyond the equivalent of their wages. This ideological, openly partisan, political concept of surplus-value and the classical labor theory of value underlying it were not discarded when Marx began pondering on a fundamental universal-scientific reinterpretation of English political economy. He retained both ideas as his central conceptual scheme.

Notes

[1] Marx (1859/1975; 1846/1968).

[2] Hegel (1958, pp. 155-207).

[3] Feuerbach (1972, pp. 154, 168, 171-172, 199, 208).

[4] Marx (1843/1975a, pp. 73, 57-100).

[5] Engels (1975, pp. 109-199, 483-487, 543-545, 570-571, 578-579).

[6] Engels (1975, p. 929).

[7] According to Hegel, both individual rights and the duties towards the state are produced in the course of a historical-developmental process of the self-realization of Objective Spirit (itself but a moment in the self-realization of Absolute Spirit) through the successive stages, or moments, of its self-estrangement, self-alienation, and objectification. Once moments of that process are self-estranged, they become objects of their own subjective activity. The organic unity and harmony of particular individual interests of civil society and those of the state, as between separate objectified moments in the self-realization of Objective Spirit, are products of subsequent acts of historical transcendence, or supersession (*Aufhebung*), whose concrete manifestations are found in medieval corporations, in the Estates and classes, as well as in various forms of legislative power.

[8] Marx (1975, pp. 207-208, 345-348, 358).

[9] Marx (1857-1858/1973, pp. 100-108).

[10] As against Marx's methodological consciousness, Echeverria (1978; 1980) demonstrated that Marx's methodical movement in *Capital* was rather a movement from the simple to the complex - rather than from the abstract to the concrete. He also demonstrated that Marx was quite ambiguous about the meaning of abstract and concrete between his 1857 "Introduction" to the *Grundrisse* and the 1859 "Preface" to *A Contribution to the Critique of Political Economy*. Echeverria reconstructed in detail the transition of Marx's thought from the logic of concrete and abstract to the logic of simple and complex as it was prompted by Hegel's *Science of Logic*. As for Marx's method proper, Echeverria only discussed the problem of the starting point in *Capital*: that of commodity vs. value.

[11] According to Marx, commodity, the simplest category of political economy, embodies four interrelated forms of value, (a) sensuously concrete use-value, or utility, as it appears in every-day use, or in consumption; (b) universal, or abstract value represented by the average socially necessary amount of abstract human labor-power expended in the production of a commodity; (c) exchange-value as the quantitative ratio of compared use-values where comparison is possible because all use-values embody abstract labor-power; and (d) general form of value expressed in gold or paper money, the special commodity chosen to serve as the measure, or equivalent of the exchange-values of all other commodities.

[12] The difference between Marx's later foursome class analysis and the crude dichotomous class division in *German Ideology* and *Communist Manifesto* is noteworthy. Marx began modifying his earlier class dichotomy already in 1848, in *Class Struggles in France*, and continued in *Eighteenth Brumaire*, but in those years he still referred to the middle classes generically as petty bourgeoisie, also including peasantry into this category.

[13] Marx (1857-1858/1973, pp. 88-100).

[14] Marx (1867/1977, pp. 125-280, 283).

[15] Marx (1867/1977, pp. 283-426, 429-639).

[16] Marx (1985/1981, p. 117).

[17] Marx (1861-1863/1971).

[18] Althusser (1965).

[19] Marx (1846/1978, pp. 136-142).

[20] Marx 1867/1977, pp. 102-103).

[21] Marx (1859/1975, p. 427).

[22] Marx (1975, pp. 421-423).

[23] Hegel (1975, pp. 111-122).

[24] For instance, by Colletti (1975, pp. 10-18).

[25] Marx (1843-1844/1975, p. 251; also 1845/1975).

[26] Marx and Engels, (1845-1846/1976, p. 356; 1975, pp. 251, 419-423; 1976a, pp. 27-30, 38-41, 57-59).

[27] Marx (1974a; 1974b).

[28] Literally, Marx spoke about the abolition of basic bourgeois institutions in the sense of their transcendental supersession, or *Aufhebung*. However, in *The German Ideology* and the *Communist Manifesto*, his usage of this term had transformed to mean destruction or annihilation rather than supersession with preservation, as it was originally meant by Hegel. This transformation of the meaning of *Aufhebung* began as early as

"On the Jewish Question," especially its second part (1843/1975c, pp. 235-241) which immediately gave Marx's writing a demagogical, anti-Semitic flavor.

29 McLelland (1970).

30 Wessel (1979), Mah (1986).

31 Marx and Engels (1845-1846/1976, pp. 38-42; 1847-1848/1974, pp. 67-68).

32 Marx (1857-1858/1973, pp. 495-497).

33 Marx (1970, pp. 50, 149, 208).

34 Marx (1867/1977, pp. 182, 489; 1894/1981, p. 278n27).

35 Marx (1974c).

36 Engels (1972).

37 Macy (1988), Cohen (1979, 1983), Ehring (1987)

38 Marx (1949/1968).

4

Western Rationalization
and Its Effects

Max Weber's work unfolded at the time of a growing influence of
Marxism that he could not ignore. One can say without exaggera-
tion that Weber's writings formed in the shadow of the profound
impact of Marxism on academic and political developments of
the early 20th century. When summarizing his life work and evi-
dently referring to Marx, Weber wrote, "Not ideas, but material
and ideal interests, directly govern men's conduct. Yet very fre-
quently the 'world images' that have been created by 'ideas' that
have, like switchmen, determined the tracks along which action
has been pushed by the dynamic of interest."[1] With the final fail-
ure of the Marxist social experiment in the Soviet Union, social
scientists lean more to the Weberian mode of analysis even
though some of it clearly bears the stamp of Marx's thought. If
we read Weber in the context of Marx's ideas that were quite influential in his time, Weber's extensive historical studies will reveal a significant conceptual contribution to today's sociology.

Weber's name is readily associated with the idea of the
Protestant ethic being closely related to the origin of modern capitalism and with a methodology of social sciences in general. We-

ber's methodology of social science is especially relevant as a guiding standard for sociologists. And yet Weber's highly nuanced positions on freedom from value judgments in social science formulated over some 13 years between 1904 and 1917 have been subjected to criticisms as well as to trivializing distortions.

The debate on this issue has not subsided to this day. While there appears to be little confusion about the meaning, for example, of instrumental and value-rationality, over and over again, commentators stress that Weber's postulate of freedom from value judgments did not mean value relativism.[2] But what did it mean, then? Is there a middle ground between objectivity and criticism? Today, the sway of political activism on U.S. university campuses is as strong as ever. Educators find themselves caught in it despite their best efforts to remain "objective." Is Weber's notion of science as a vocation still meaningful in today's world? Was Weber himself consistent and "objective" in applying his historic concept of vocation to social realities of modern times? And what is the use of his celebrated value-rationality if it cannot help directing our social lives? Let us re-read Weber from this perspective and see if we can find answers to these questions.

Economic Rationality as Religious Value

It is widely accepted that the main theme of Weber's substantive sociology is the increasing rationalization of Western societies, and that the thematic unity of Weber's life work is contained in his monumental *Economy and Society*. Seidman added the sociology of religion as the substantive material equally essential for understanding Weber's entire project.[3] Tenbruck goes even further by limiting Weber's central substantive program to his sociology of religion beginning with *Protestant Ethic* - rather than *Economy and Society*.[4] Tenbruck points out that *Economy and Society* is mostly a collection of unfinished manuscripts put together and posthumously published to fulfill Weber's contractual obligations.

According to Tenbruck, the process of disenchantment described in *The Protestant Ethic* marked the end of the first stage in the overall Western rationalization process. It continued as the process of modernization. While disenchantment only meant an emancipation of economic ethic from magic and mysticism, modernization involves progressive rationality of social action. Indeed, as it is clear from Weber's "Social Psychology of the World Religions" and from *Ancient Judaism,* the origins of Western rationality go back to ancient Judaism. It was by following the model of rational Judaism, that the ascetic Protestant ethic fostered a belief that the possession of grace necessary for salvation could be achieved through value-rational economic action. This rationality was developed within religion rather than against it. What exactly was the social meaning of the value-rationality of ancient Judaism, and how was it transformed in modern Western religious beliefs and practices?

Weber's answer to this question was centered on the idea of social justice. The Israelite prophets saw social injustice that violated the spirit of the Mosaic Law only as a motive of God's wrath, not as the cause or a program of social reform. Yet, justice meant some kind of compensation or reward for one's good deeds and punishment for other's injustice. Such calculable expectations of just compensation are widely diffused in all religions of the world today. Ancient Jews anticipated their salvation through a revolution of prevailing social stratification for the sake of God's people who had been chosen and called not to a pariah position but to one of prestige. Jewish religion thus became a religion of retribution. God's Commandments were observed for the sake of a hope of compensation. From such a compensatory hope the Jews were bound to derive new strength, consciously or unconsciously.[5]

Since Christianity, especially Protestantism, inherited these Jewish ideas, Weber concluded that Western conceptions of the world showed a similar need for a rational interpretation of "the distribution of fortunes among men." As the religious and ethical reflections upon the world were increasingly rationalized and primitive magical notions removed, "the theodicy of suffering encountered increasing difficulties." There was a need to measure the status of (economically) successful and unsuccessful people with the same yardstick. It was understood then that "those strata which were 'satiated' and favored in this world had only a small urge to be saved." Salvation was much more important for those who were "less socially valued." Ethical prophecies nourished the sense of dignity among the socially disadvantaged and a sense that "their worth is guaranteed or constituted by an *ethical imperative,* or by their own functional *achievement.*"[6]

Following this logic of the economic rationality of religion, Weber expanded his approach to all other Western institutions and to major world cultures as typical forms of social order. Any social order is based on lower strata accepting the domination of upper ones as legitimate. In Weber's social genesis, in the beginning, there was domination of and by charisma. The charismatic form of legitimate authority was based on purely individual qualities of natural leaders and the devotion of the followers. Charismatic authority is always revolutionary and, by the same token, very unstable.[7] By way of routinization, the charismatic form of domination was then transformed into the traditional one and, finally, into the modern legal-bureaucratic type. Apparently, Weber was following here the ideas of his neo-Kantian friend and "first-rate stimulator" Georg Simmel.[8]

All other types of legitimate authority fall as fluid transitional types between these pure types about which Weber spoke in the Logos essay.[9] Thus, European feudalism was an unsuccessful variety of patrimonial domination, itself a temporary historic form of charismatic authority in the process of routinization.[10] The young socialism of the early 20th century was also a form of revolutionary charismatic authority in the process of transformation into direct, or immediate plebiscitary democracy.[11] The administrative system adopted by the Estates was an underdeveloped form of bureaucracy - charismatic domination in the process of rationalization.[12]

Of the three pure types of domination, bureaucracy became a special focus of Weber's attention. As Weber saw it, the actions of bureaucratic officials are regulated by rules, such as laws of the state or administrative regulations of organizations. There are rules for all occasions: rules that regulate the employment of personnel according to pre-set criteria of qualification; rules regarding the application of coercive means in case of an infraction of rules; rules clearly specifying the hierarchical system of subordination and appeal, and many others. Bureaucracy presupposes a separation of private concerns from public ones. Private residence, private correspondence, private assets, and private time are all strictly segregated from the official ones. If a conflict arises between the two, it is resolved in the interest of official duties.[13]

The stratification of any social order includes both classes and status groups. Unlike organized status groups, classes are more "amorphous," they are defined by common external properties that give ground for claiming privileges. Status stratification becomes favored when "bases of acquisition and distribution of goods are stable." Classes come to the fore in times of technological and economic transformation. Often both types of social stratification overlap.[14]

Understanding Historical Individuals

According to Weber, the validity and stability of social order is maintained either internally – by custom and fashion – or externally – by convention and law. These guarantees of legitimate domination maintain uniformity of ways in which individual social actions are oriented. The three main historic types of orientation of social action – affective, habitual, and rational – parallel the three pure historic types of legitimate domination – charismatic, traditional, and legal-bureaucratic. Rational orientation of action falls into two subtypes – instrumental and value-rational. In this way guaranteed uniformity of individual action orientations ensures that social relationships become "guided by a belief in the existence of legitimate order." And it is only to the extent that actors have such a belief that any social order is legitimate and valid.[15]

Value-rationality is not given to an observer as lying on the surface of individual actions. Since any such observation must itself be non-judgmental, i.e., value-neutral, the value-rationality of economic or other conduct can only be revealed by interpretive understanding. This same principle applies to the work of a historic sociologist conceptualizing and explaining these phenomena. According to Weber, a social scientist faced with the task of conceptualizing historical material begins by limiting the infinite mass of available documents by selectively isolating "historical individuals," those fragments of documentary historical evidence that are considered important, or significant. The selection of such "unique configurations of factors" that are then placed within a wider historical context is guided by the (intuitive) sense of universal cultural values that are presumed to be embodied in the historical individuals.[16] Next, the sociologist must actually present the historical individuals as relevant to the values that guided his choice. This is what Weber called interpretive understanding (*Verstehen*).[17]

The facts comprising historical individuals can be valued not only "for their own sake," but also as secondary facts shedding light on primary ones. Such secondary historical facts are, above all, those that precede primary facts in time and that can be interpreted as their causes. The tracing of primary historical individuals to their origin in such a causal regress, i.e., explanation, is an integral if subordinate part of their understanding.[18] Interpretive understanding is achieved by presenting all selected historical individuals as value-relevant, as having a certain universal significance. The universal significance of historical individuals is derived from their orientation to certain "rules of historical process," rules that are erroneously called laws in economics. This significance is contained in the knowledge of "the ways people tend to act in specific life situations," the ways that are either actually recognized as universally valid, or at least supposed to be recognized as such. This is what Weber held as the knowledge of regularities in historical process.[19]

What Weber had in mind was Rickert's ultimate, transcendental, metahistorical values that represent the universally significant in cultural sciences as against unique, individual, subjective, and relativistic historical individuals. However, Weber stopped short of such a straightforward formulation. Instead, he discussed the problem of the objectivity of cultural sciences in terms of grounds for a choice between different value-relevances. This position opened the door to the problem of distinguishing between objective and so-called subjective value-relevance which undermined Weber's overall solution to the neo-Kantian dilemma of individualizing versus generalizing sciences as is demonstrated in the debate on this issue.[20]

Thus understood selected historical individuals are to be reconstructed into a still smaller number of ideal types - imaginary models, or limiting cases that present a "synthesis of those traits which are common to numerous concrete [historical] phenomena." Ideal types give an ideal picture of events, a "conceptual construct that is neither historical reality, nor even the 'true' reality." They are utopias in this sense whose primary role is to bring together certain relationships and events of historical life into a complex conceived to be an internally consistent system. Ideal types are systematically defined "genetic concepts," and for that reason they can be used to bring an order into what otherwise is "a chaos of infinitely differentiated and highly contradictory complexes of ideas and feelings." Precise concepts of these imaginary models form a "categorial construct, [...] a firm skeleton of causal reasoning." The content of such pure ideal types differs from the substantively rich historical reality they represent. They must not be treated as a procrustean bed for history or hypostatized as its motive forces.[21] Consequently, Weber warned against equating ideal-typical historical reconstructions with actual historical processes "thought of as an 'object' governed by deterministic laws."

Having performed in thought the "analysis and isolation of the constituents of what is immediately given, seen as a complex of possible causal relationships," the historian judges various probable courses of "what would have happened if certain conditions had been eliminated or altered." Following the von Kries-Radbruch controversy in German jurisprudence, Weber distinguished two types of historical causality: (a) "adequate causation" by objectively possible social conditions to be conceived - in the most rational case - in terms of ideal types to which certain concrete events can be subsumed as being alike, i.e., adequate to each other, and (b) "chance causation" by natural or unpredictable, unique, truly historic events whose meaning must be considered in their own terms. The latter type is accidental with respect to the objective probabilities reflected in ideal types, but it is an equally important "causal factor in a concrete historical complex."[22] Social action may be responsible for chance causation of historical facts. Such action can be produced by a single agent or by an anthropocentric "plurality of agents conceived as a group" that is not an impersonal "mass of people." Hence the importance of biography in historical sciences that can account for certain chance components of events. Biography presents the intrinsic nature of a personality that is of more than just a literary interest. It can reveal historic events and other relevant facts as source material for historical interpretation.[23]

Furthermore, in his analytical and synthesizing work, a historian proceeds "in much the same way as the historical individual himself." Like any historical agent, an historian also assesses various possible causal configurations in his factual material that set the conditions for his creative imagination, and similarly hopes for success. Any historian and any scholar in the cultural-historical sciences in general is himself a valuing and judging social actor as is the historical agent who constitutes the subject-matter of his professional scholarly work. However, there is also a significant difference between the positions of these two social actors. Prospectively, the historical agent, including the historian himself, acts regarding the expected future outcome of his work on the basis of his judgment of the probability of and a hope for success. By contrast, the outcome of the action of the historical agent constituting the subject-matter of scholarly historical work is known in advance as an accomplished fact. That outcome is usually a success so long as history is primarily concerned with cultural excellences.[24]

There are two major implications of this difference between the two positions. One is the variety in the degrees of rationality that can be attributed to a social actor. While the retrospective position can be described as the most rational one - being synonymous with any scientific world outlook - the prospective position of both a historian and of his subject-matter can be anything between the poles of maximum rationality and maximum non-rationality, none of which prevents it, however, from being understood and interpreted in terms of a science of social action. The other implication is that glossing over the difference between the two positions - the prospective and the retrospective one - is detrimental to the results of scholarly work both in terms of its internal logic and of its chances for success. It was in view of this difference that Weber called for a total separation of the domain of values from empirical social science.[25]

These sciences can help understand the origins of social phenomena, but they can say nothing about their value for us. Professors should not give their personal opinions about possible political impact of such phenomena in the classroom. They should rather teach students how to recognize "inconvenient facts." There is a plurality of values in the world, and their conflict cannot be reconciled. One can only strive to understand the meaning of all these values. Students should not expect a professor to be a political leader. The practical value of social science is not in its practical applications, but in developing methods of thought, in giving students clarity of mind, and in fostering scholarly integrity. In short, science is a vocation. "No science is absolutely free from presuppositions, and no science can prove its fundamental value to the man who rejects these presuppositions.

The meaning of some of these presuppositions has origins in theology that has undergone a process of rationalization."[26]

Critical Evaluation of Modernity

Weber voiced a deep pessimism about the consequences of the historic processes of Western rationalization. Instead of a methodical value-rational way of life in pursuit of a vocation, he saw "specialists without spirit and sensualists without heart" in the modern world. Or, in the words of the new translation of *The Protestant Ethic*, "Victorious capitalism [...] ever since it came to rest on a mechanical foundation, no longer needs asceticism as a supporting pillar. Even the optimistic temperament of asceticism's joyful heir, the Enlightenment, appears to be fading. And the idea of an 'obligation to search for and then accept a vocational calling' now wanders around in our lives as the ghost of beliefs no longer anchored in the substance of religion."[27] Clearly, Weber's critical observation about modern outcomes of the rationalization process implied unfulfilled value-rationality of rule-governed, institutional collective practices. What he saw instead was the instrumental rationality of self-interest and cost-benefit calculus, a rationality of power relationships and social inequality.[28] He observed an ethic of success rather than of responsibility.[29] But what was the presupposition of Weber's own value-judgment about modern rationalization? What was the ideal standard against which he judged modernity? In other words, what was the rationality of Weber's own social action as a sociologist?

Weber's critique of the modern rationalization process was a value-judgment, but not about a unique historical individual. Rather, it was about the lack of collective practices governed by ethical cultural norms that he expected to find in his time, but could not. He was projecting the ideal-type of value-rationality from the past onto modern times. The unique cultural value on which Weber's sociology of *The Protestant Ethic* was based was social justice derived from his analysis of ancient Judaism. This same value was the standard on which Weber's critical evaluation of modern social reality was based. And this is exactly the kind of value-rationality students expect to hear from professors in the classroom and readers expect to see in scholarly books and papers. What students and readers look for is a connection between abstract categories used in social science and certain social-cultural values on which they are ultimately based. They look for a connection between thin abstractions that are meaningful to their professors and notions that are self-evident or at least familiar to them. Weber's idea of a social science as a vocation may have been value-neutral in the sense of his contemporary political ideologies, but it was not free from all values, after all.

Ultimately, all abstract notions of social sciences are relevant to some values or others. Weber's concept of modern rationalization was in fact an abstraction of social justice as a unique social value. Vocation was an abstraction of the same value. And so was disenchantment. And so was economic ethic. It is the separation of these abstractions from their roots in historic social values that is responsible for the perception of Weber's ambivalence noted by many commentators.[30] While instrumental and value-rationality were conceived by Weber as coequal ideal types, value-rationality turns out to be more abstract than rationality of the instrumental kind. Modern social reality could be characterized by various degrees of instrumental rationality, but value-rationality served as a standard against which the realities of modern social stratification could be evaluated. In advancing his thesis of the highly ethical religious origins of modern capitalism, Weber realized that capitalism also had an ugly side. Thus Weber's significant social action of a sociologist was more than abstracting ideal types from historical individuals. He was also using them as standards for evaluating modernity.

One implication of this view is that deviations of instrumentally oriented action and of their results from standards of value-rationality and of its outcomes can be for the better or for the worse. Indeed, as the modern type of domination, legal bureaucracy is unequalled in the optimal performance of specialized administrative functions according to purely objective considerations, i.e., according to calculable rules and without regard for persons. "Bureaucracy develops more perfectly the more it is 'dehumanized', the more completely it succeeds in eliminating from official business love, hatred, and all purely personal, irrational, and emotional elements which escape calculation." Like a well-lubricated machine, bureaucracy secures "precision, speed, unambiguity [...], unity, strict subordination, reduction of friction and of material and personal costs."[31]

Still, Weber was tenuous and limited when crossing the line between social history as causal explanation of historical individuals and sociology as a science of evaluating the outcomes of historical development. For all his refined methodology of evaluating social reality in terms of ideal types, ideal types remained but servants of history for him. Weber believed that an "analytical ordering of social reality" was the true objective of any social science, and he spoke about "the imperative need to operate with unambiguous concepts which are not only particularly but also systematically defined," as well as about the need for such concepts to form "an internally consistent system."[32] On the other hand, he vehemently opposed any "systematic science of culture" not only in the sense of "definitive, objectively valid, systematic fixation of the problems which it should treat, [but also as] a closed system of concepts in which reality is synthesized in some sort of permanently and universally valid classification." [33]

Weber turned to sociology from economic and legal history where he showed strong leanings towards Simmel's and Rickert's philosophy and methodology of history as against both the "irrationality" of Ranke's descriptive-historicist school and the absolute rationality of Hegel's "emanatism." He differentiated between history and sociology rather late in his career, only in the prefatory methodological section of Part One of *Economy and Society* written about 1918. There he declared that unlike history "which is oriented to the causal analysis and explanation of individual actions, structures and personalities possessing cultural significance, [sociology] seeks to formulate type concepts and generalized uniformities of empirical process. [And although] the empirical material which underlies the concepts of sociology consists to a very large extent [...] of the same concrete processes of action which are dealt with by historians, [its task in forming concepts and generalizations is only to make a contribution] toward the causal explanation of some historically and culturally important phenomenon."[34]

Weber was much more involved with historical methodology than with principles of sociology that occupied a rather auxiliary role in his work. His own understanding of historical individuals preceding their ideal-typical interpretation was even more involved with a professional historian's attitude and stance.[35] The somewhat blurred distinction between the historical and the sociological in Weber's actual work had a reverse effect, too. As he was more concerned with history than with sociology, he did not see any need to connect his professed "understanding sociology" and explanation of historic facts by adequate and chance causes. Jaspers observed that Weber approached each period of the past as a contemporary one.[36] Based on such an "understanding," and relying on the conceptual scheme constructed with dichotomous categories, Weber was inescapably limited in his sociological work proper in fulfilling the promise of his own methodological principles.

Note

[1] Weber (1915/1946a).
[2] For example, Blum (1944), Portis (1980).
[3] Seidman (1984).
[4] Tenbruck (1980).
[5] Weber (1917-1920/1967).
[6] Weber (1915/1946a, pp. 275-276). "The closest connection between ethical religion and rational economic development - particularly capitalism - was effected by all the forms of ascetic Protestantism and sectarianism in both Western and Eastern Europe [... However,] only in the Occident was the additional step taken [...] of transferring rational asceticism into the life of the world. [...An] unbroken unity integrating in systematic fashion an ethic of vocation in the world with assurance of religious salvation was the unique creation of ascetic Protestantism alone. Furthermore, only in the Protestant ethic of vocation does the world, despite all its creaturely imperfections, possess unique and religious significance as the object through which one fulfills his duties by

rational behavior accounting to the will of an absolutely transcendental god" (1922/1978, pp. 479, 555-556).

[7] Weber (1922/1978, pp. 1111-1120).

[8] Weber (1972, p. 158). According to Simmel (1950, pp. 181-189), behind the seemingly one-sided relationship of domination and subordination there is actually a reciprocal social interaction in which those ruled have "a considerable measure of personal freedom." Every domination, Simmel argued, is based on a "more or less voluntary faith" of the subjected party, including subordination to law. Simmel also spoke of authority in this connection. He distinguished between authority coming from super-individual social institutions like the state, the church, the school, or the military organization, etc., by virtue of occupying an official position in them, on the one hand, and authority coming from the person himself, from his personal prestige. Consequently, Simmel introduced a three-fold typology of subordination: subordination under an individual, subordination under a group, and subordination under an objective principle. Weber's three types of domination are easily recognizable here.

[9] Weber (1913/1981, pp. 154, 160, 161, 171).

[10] Weber (1922/1978, pp. 246-266, 1070, 1121-1123).

[11] Weber (1922/1978, pp. 266-271, 1126-1128; 1924/1971, pp. 191-219).

[12] Weber (1913/1981, pp. 154, 160, 161, 171; 1922/1978, pp. 1085-1087, 1116-1117).

[13] Weber (1922/1978, pp. 956-958).

[14] Weber (1922/1978, pp. 305-307, 932-938).

[15] Weber (1922/1978, pp. 22-38).

[16] Weber (1903-1907/1975, p. 173; 1904/1949, pp. 72-81).

[17] Occasionally, Weber implied a distinction between subjective and objective understanding in Simmel's sense, but on the whole, he followed Rickert's idea of value-relevant understanding (cf. 1903-1907/1975, pp. 152-154, and 1913/1981, p. 151).

[18] Weber (1906/1949, pp. 135, 143-144, 155-156, 160-161; 1906/1978, pp. 121, 125; 1914/1978, p. 80).

[19] Weber (1903-1907/1975, pp. 96, 102, 123, 173; 1904/1949, pp. 79-80, 93, 111).

[20] See Oakes (1988a, 1988b), Wagner and Zipprian (1988).

[21] Weber (1903-1907/1975, pp. 125-129, 152-162, 174-176, 182-186; 1904/1949, pp. 54-55, 76-84, 90-94, 111-112; 1906/1949, pp. 143-160; 1906/1978, pp. 115-122; 1914/1978, pp. 87-88). While all other categories introduced by Weber – types of legitimate domination, of social action and its orientation - are purely ideal types, the two stages of Western rationalization are historically real (Tenbruck 1980).

[22] Weber (1903-1907/1975, pp. 98-100; 1906/1978, pp. 120, 124, 127; 1922/1978, p. xliv).

[23] Weber (1903-1907/1975, pp. 98-100, 102-103, 239n13; 1906/1949, pp. 137-142).

[24] Weber (1903-1907/1975, p.98; 1906/1978, p. 112; Rickert, 1962, p. 22).

[25] Weber wrote (1903-1907/1975, pp. 125-129), "The constant confusion of the scientific discussion of facts and their evaluation is still one of the most widespread and one of the most damaging traits of work in our field. [...] Concern on the part of history to judge historical actions as responsible before the conscience of history [...] would suspend its character as an empirical science." And again, "[...] anyone engaged in research or in presenting its results should keep [the] two things absolutely separate, be-

cause they involve different kinds of problem. [...] The validity of a practical imperative as a norm, on the one hand, and the truth claim of a statement of empirical fact, on the other, creates problems at totally different levels, and [...] the specific value of each of them will be diminished if this is not recognized." Similarly in 1904/1949, pp. 60, 81-84, 123-124; 1906/1978, p. 112; 1914/1978, pp. 76, 78-79, 97.

[26] Weber (1917/1946).

[27] Weber (1920/2002, p. 124).

[28] Cohen (2000). Along with "action," the term "conduct" is routinely used by Weber - rather than "behavior" to avoid implying behaviorism unconcerned with motives and subjective meanings. Weber specifically differentiated this usage in the opening of *Economy and Society*. But the difference between (ends-and-means rationally) meaningful conduct and behavior is very thin in English. For all practical purposes these two terms are synonymous. That is why they are routinely used as interchangeable in commentaries on Weber.

[29] In terms of Weber's biographical background, instrumental rationality meant his father's "ethic of success" as opposed to his mother's "ethic of conscience" (Marianne Weber, 1975).

[30] Bendix (1962), Mitzman (1970), Oakes (1982), Portis (1986).

[31] Weber (1922/1978, pp. 223-226, 973-975, 987).

[32] Weber (1904/1949, pp. 58, 63, 90, 93)

[33] Weber (1904/1949, p. 84).

[34] Weber (1922/1978, pp. 19-20).

[35] Cf. Whimster (1980).

[36] Jaspers (1964, p. 238).

5

From Mechanical to Organic Solidarity

Emile Durkheim became an advocate of a science of sociology in his early adulthood. Social meant moral for him, and sociology was identical with a science of morality. Unlike the moralists and philosophers who advanced traditional or preconceived notions about morality, Durkheim wished to discover moral truths and even laws about society that were amenable to demonstrable proof or refutation. Inspired by Spencer's and Comte's ideas of social evolution, differentiation and integration, Durkheim started from a belief that valid social-scientific knowledge could be an integral part of morality itself. He believed that moral education based on findings of such a science would promote social discipline, autonomy of the individual, and liberate his will.

Out of this conviction Durkheim proclaimed the need to disengage rational morality from religion with which it was fused, so that it could be given a firm foundation in social science. In such a science, there would be no place for any religious subject-matter in its own right.[1] And yet, the second half of Durkheim's intellectual career was mostly devoted to the sociology of religion. In "The Evolution of Punishment" he even spoke of religious criminality as more offensive to collective conscience than simple "human criminality." [2] Is there then any thematic unity in Durkheim's intellectual legacy?

Social Solidarity and Law

In his doctoral dissertation, Durkheim set out to investigate the functions of the division of labor in late 19th-century Europe and America characterized by progressive diversity and complexity brought about by rapid industrialization processes. What Durkheim meant by the functions of the division of labor was its useful social, i.e., moral outcomes as opposed to purely technical or economic ones. Along with the benefits of increased productivity and professional specialization associated with the division of labor, Durkheim noted numerous labor disputes, business failures causing industrial and commercial crises. The beneficial social effects of the division of labor were in the exchange of complementary functions among dissimilar groups of people as well as among individuals. The result was a social organism of which sexual division of labor and the family institution was a good model.

Thus viewed, the economic effects of the division of labor are "insignificant compared with the moral effect that it produces, and its true function is to create between two or more people a feeling of solidarity." The real function of the division of labor is "in its moral character, since needs for order, harmony and social solidarity are generally reckoned to be moral ones."[3] The French term "*solidarité morale*" was used in the sense of social cohesion and interdependence. Durkheim also meant a social bond by it as used by a contemporary German social theorist Albert Schaeffle.[4] Since social solidarity as the sum total of social bonds could not be directly observed and measured within the framework of social science, Durkheim referred to law and custom as their (partial and imperfect, yet objective and quantifiable) indicators. Law regulates social relationships and "reproduces the main forms of social solidarity." It is only necessary to "classify the different types of law in order to be able to investigate which types of social solidarity correspond to them."

Durkheim distinguished between repressive (criminal) and retributive (civil, administrative, etc.) law. These two types of law were closely related, even combined, but their relative weight changed historically. The rules of criminal and civil law were taken as indicators and external symbols of mechanical and organic social solidarity, respectively. As societies become more complex and more organized in the course of social evolution, civil retribution becomes more prevalent than criminal punishment, and "social discipline [...] loses more and more its authoritarian rigor."[5] Therefore, Durkheim concluded, progressive division of labor produces organic social solidarity which, unlike the mechanical, direct solidarity of primitive and ancient societies devoid of any significant division of labor, binds modern society indirectly, through its members' specialized contributions to a common good.

The primitive morality of mechanical solidarity "constitutes a category of rules where the idea of authority plays an absolutely preponderant role [...The] moral rule consists entirely in a commandment and in nothing else. [...This] kind of morality [...] is a system of commandments."[6] Mechanical solidarity is indicated by punishment for crimes defined as acts offensive to "strong, well-defined states of collective consciousness." The latter is the "totality of beliefs and sentiments common to the average members of a society."[7] Mechanical solidarity means conformity of each individual conscience in a society to the same collective conscience. Retributive law indicative of organic solidarity does not involve collective conscience common to all members of society, but it does not amount to arbitration of private interests either. By awarding damages in restoring real rights or personal privileges, retributive law is still involved to a greater or smaller extent in terms of particular parts of collective conscience that may be common to the interests and rights disputed by parties to a civil action.

Unlike the uniform and direct role of mechanical solidarity, (this negative) organic solidarity links members of society in a multitude of highly differentiated, particular ways. Positive organic solidarity is produced by domestic, contractual, commercial, administrative, and constitutional law through restoring cooperation among parties to a dispute. It is this latter, positive type of organic solidarity that is directly related to the division of labor in society. Since members of society choose their own particular spheres of action, collective conscience penetrates only to the extent of practices common to particular professions.[8]

Durkheim endorsed Gaston Richard's views on the origins of the idea of law.[9] Like Durkheim, G. Richard rejected individualist utilitarian theories of law based on the idea of self-interested conduct. Rather, he associated law with the idea of social justice achieved within the framework of the arbitration institution where "individual appetites" are subsumed to the (institutionalized) social goals of "protection against mutual destruction." The institution of law exists primarily in the consciousness of members of society, and only secondarily in the formal judicial arrangements of the state. Arbitration will "check and ward off [the] excesses" of committed offenses, and its outcomes must be guaranteed to the victim "without the guilty party being able to abridge it. [...] The State, once constituted, can render the carrying out of this guarantee more regular, but it does not create it. It has its roots in the very *conscience* of societies." In this concept an offense is not a violation of the law, as is usually thought. On the contrary, the law as a fundamental idea is a social response to offense. For the law to be, sociability and charity must exist first. Without them, no arbitration can be guaranteed. "[L]aw is born out of our feeling of solidarity against [unjust, Hobbesian] war."[10]

Organic social solidarity is produced in the normal course of the division of labor. But that is only an ideal state of affairs. In reality, the division of labor takes abnormal forms where hostility and conflicts reign rather than social solidarity. Abnormal forms of the division of labor, anomic in particular, distort and undermine organic solidarity which leads to conflicts between labor and capital as well as to marital divorce. Industrial and commercial crises, bankruptcies and business failures are anomic violations of the moral principle of organic solidarity. Unlike medieval trade guilds where workmen "led the same existence" as their master, a deep gulf separates them in the modern industrial world. The working masses are separated from their bosses in both salaries and working conditions. The "habits and rules" that once applied equally to the master and his apprentice and differed only depending on their professional standing, have now gone their separate ways.

In modern society "this tension in social relationships is due in part to the fact that workers do not really desire the status (*la condition*) assigned to them and too often accept them only under constraint and force, not having any means of gaining any other conditions."[11] Something similar happens in the realm of science where individual scholars may produce empirical works of limited interest that are not coordinated with the general condition of their particular discipline let alone the edifice of science as a whole.[12] Durkheim then highlighted the ideas of debt and its repayment in the operation of thus understood social justice. Both civil and criminal offenses can be seen as debt - debt to private parties in the case of civil offenses and debt to society in the case of criminal ones. Criminal offenses disturb social order in its entirety which gives rise to the institution of criminal punishment. The idea of social solidarity prevails in both cases.

Anomie and Social Justice

What is violated in anomic division of labor and what fails to produce organic solidarity among occupational groups is a lack of coordination between the functions of such groups as certain "ways of acting," on the one hand, and "general conditions of life," on the other. Where such a coordination does exist, the "relationship entertained between these functions cannot […] fail to arrive at the same level of stability and regularity." Repeated habits of such coordination become rules of conduct.[13] Anomic division of labor is a result of lack of regulation coordinating, for example, the number of business undertakings in each branch of industry so that it might correspond to levels of consumption in their particular areas of economic life. This does not have to be achieved by a restricting legislation. Regular and harmonious performance of social functions can be achieved in other ways. Such equilibrium may restore itself without outside intervention in private enterprise through the balance of supply and demand. However, this does not happen immediately, but rather after more or less prolonged disturbances. The progress of the division of labor, of its functional specialization and overall complexity may also make such disturbances more numerous. This is the state of anomie.[14]

In *Suicide* anomie was also understood as absence of regulation of human conduct based on the principle of social justice. "In normal conditions the collective order is regarded as just by the great majority of persons." Individuals "cannot assign themselves this law of justice, [...] society alone can play this moderating role." Ultimately, organic social solidarity is achieved by our collective conscience of what is just. Aspirations for social justice anticipate "the normal state to come." These trends "are necessary consequences of the changes that have taken place in the structure of societies."[15]

Social justice consists in a harmony between a hierarchy of occupational groups fulfilling different social functions and a hierarchy of limits placed on the satisfaction of human needs depending on their natural talents and other merits. It would be "of little use for everyone to recognize the justice of the hierarchy of functions established by public opinion, if he did not also consider the distribution of these functions just." But in times of social upheavals such as economic crises or abrupt transitions "something like a declassification occurs which suddenly casts certain individuals into a lower state than their previous one, "and this is followed by "rises in the curve of suicides." Higher suicide rates are also related to anomic family relations as indicated by the statistics of divorce. [16] Durkheim further developed the theme of social justice as the foundation of social order in *Professional Ethic*, in *Socialism and Saint-Simon*, and in *Moral Education* where it was contrasted with charity.

Durkheim criticized socialists and Marx for responding emotionally rather than scientifically to prevailing social injustices. While also critical of modern capitalist society, Durkheim stood for social reforms rather than sweeping and destructive social revolution sought by Marx and his followers. He objected to their idea of social equality without merit comparing it to charity.[17] Instead, Durkheim advocated justice as social action to be administered by the state. "Charity has moral value only as a symptom of a moral state with which it is associated; because it points to a moral propensity [...] to go beyond one's self, to go beyond the circle of self-interest, it clears the way for a true morality."[18]

Having in mind his concept of mechanical solidarity, he compared Marx's primitive communism to Tönnies' *Gemeinschaft* and characterized both as describing the primeval stage of human social evolution.[19] Durkheim also disagreed with Marx's atheist materialist conception of history. In a significant passage that rehabilitated religion as a subject-matter of sociological study he said, "Sociologists and historians tend increasingly to come together in their common affirmation that religion [rather than economic interests] is the most primitive of all social phenomena. It is from it that have emerged, through successive transformations, all the other manifestations of collective activity – law, morality, art, science, political forms, etc. In principle, everything is religious."[20]

Sacred Beliefs and Practices

Durkheim's sociology of religion was a direct continuation of his sociology of secular morality. He wrote about religion already in *The Division of Labor*[21] and much earlier,[22] but it was after 1895 that his life was marked by a "feverish activity"[23] of a thorough sociological study of primitive religion. In "Sociology and the Social Sciences" co-authored with Paul Fouconnet, already at the Sorbonne, Durkheim appreciated the great volume of comparative studies of religion in ethnography and anthropology as demonstrating "the uniformity of religious beliefs and practices over the whole humanity," and the linking of "the religions of the most highly cultured societies and those of the lowest tribes, [...] each serving mutually to explain the other."[24] In "Individual and Collective Representations," he outlined a theory of the origin of modern religious beliefs in collective representations as modeled after the morphological social structure of primitive clans.[25] According to Durkheim, modern complex myths, theogonies, and cosmologies evolved from primitive collective representations but subsequently lost connection with the social structures of their origin.

By that time, Durkheim had also published the first volume of *L'Anneé sociologique* where special attention was given to reviewing works on the origin of the family and totemism.[26] In his paper "Concerning the Definition of Religious Phenomena," Durkheim spoke about religious phenomena to be studied as external facts. He stressed the obligatory character of religious beliefs and practices characterizing both as sacred. Durkheim proposed that since society and religion were inseparable in ancient times, individual rights emphasized in modernity had their origin in sacred objects of religious worship. Today's appropriation of these objects by individuals, e.g., private property, was originally a social concession, and its practice on a wide scale would be unthinkable in ancient times as profanation. Along the same lines, Durkheim interpreted ancient gods as "collective forces personified and hypostatized in material form."[27] When in "Value Judgments and Judgments of Reality,"[28] written already after *The Elementary Forms*, Durkheim spoke about "collective ferment," he was talking about the same mechanism of the origin of modern social institutions. Earlier versions of the same idea included the "love of society" in "The Determination of Moral Facts,"[29] and "attachment to the group" in *Moral Education*.

Between 1895 and 1906, Durkheim wrote some 25 smaller articles and reviews on religion for *L'Anneé sociologique*, including many on totemism.[30] In "The Determination of Moral Facts" read in 1906, Durkheim again spoke about the authority of modern society replacing that of God, and about individual moral conscience as the subjective element of social authority. He also noted the difficulty of dissociating modern morality from religion.[31] All these partial formulations of Durkheim's sociology of religion since 1895 were brought together in his lectures of 1906-1907. Five years later they were published as *The Elementary Forms of the Religious Life*. Thus Durkheim completed a full circle in his attitude to religion: from its rejection in adolescence for the sake of a social science to an acceptance in the form of rational social science in his mature years.

The Elementary Forms distinguished between religious beliefs and religious ritual practices. Religious beliefs were defined as beliefs in the sacred, i.e., in ideal and transcendental dogmas. These were contrasted with profane objects, "those to which [...] interdictions are applied and which must remain at a distance from the first." Religious rites were "the rules of conduct which prescribe how a man should comport himself in the presence of these sacred objects." The sacred is to profane as absolute is to relative. Both religious beliefs and ritual practices were differentiated from individualistic magical ones by the association of the former with the moral social community of a Church. To lead a more religious life one must withdraw from the profane world, such as into a monastery. A complete religiosity means asceticism, "for the only manner of fully escaping the profane life, is, after all, to forsake all life."

Finally, Durkheim defined primitive society by identifying it with the social structure of a clan, and its primitive religion, with the worship of sacred animals and plants, i.e., with totemism. Thus the problem of studying the elementary forms of religious life was narrowed to the analysis of totemism in primitive clans for which the empirical data were provided by observations of British and American anthropologists of the aboriginal tribes of Central Australia and North-American Indians.[32] The primitive religious beliefs were originally produced by the "general, or collective effervescence"[33] of a clan which "dynamogenically" elevated believers above their profane individual existences to a sacred social one.[34] The effervescence was translated into obligatory primitive ritual practices that were essential for periodically "giving direction" to the religious community.[35] These "effervescent assemblies" gave a forceful and coercive reconfirmation of the morality of the social group.

When in monotheistic religions the multiplicity of gods was reduced to one, the one supreme God symbolized the unity of society, of the social group, of its sacredness, and its moral authority over the individual member as well as the object of his aspirations.[36] "To attribute certain things in nature to a god amounts to the same thing as to group them under the same generic rubric, or to place them in the same class; and the genealogies and identifications relating divinities to each other imply relations of co-ordination or subordination between the classes of things represented by these divinities."[37] According to this sociology of knowledge, all human concepts were originally such collective representations that later became fixed, immutable, universal, and superimposed on our individual experience in the course of a long historical evolution.[38] Eventually, they become external to individual consciousness, "social products of the second degree."[39]

Thus primitive conceptual classifications were originally modeled on the structures of social relations within primitive tribes, clans, etc. Those classifications were eventually purified and systematized within the disciplined thought of ancient Greek philosophy where they became the logical categories of our thought that have shown a remarkable resistance to change.[40] Furthermore, all mythologies are fundamentally such classifications based on authoritative religious beliefs. *The Elementary Forms* reiterated Durkheim's earlier thesis about the eternal nature of religion along with his predictions of the humanistic religion of the future.[41] Only occasionally did he return to the theme of modern morality and organic solidarity after that - as in the Preface to the second edition of *The Division of Labor* and in *Professional*

Ethics.[42] *Suicide* was published two years after the revelation of 1895, but it had been in the making for about a decade, at least since "Suicide and Birth-rate" published in 1888.

Observing and Explaining Social Facts

In Durkheim's design, general sociology would subsume the subject-matters of traditional social sciences such as political economy and ethnology by giving them a unified framework but without destroying their valid achievements.[43] That unified framework fell into two related subdivisions, one studying demographic and institutional aspects of social facts, and the other, their social functions. Following a biological model only slightly modified since Spencer, Durkheim called the former subdivision social morphology and the latter, social psychology. Morphological-institutional social structures are characterized by "their total lack of material substance." They form unities of diversity that "place society in harmony within itself and with the outside world."[44] Durkheim devoted his main attention to social functions. It was in the discovery of the laws governing the functioning of (moral) social facts that he saw the primary task for nascent sociology.[45]

Social facts are facts because they are external to individuals, and they are social because they are characteristic of human collectivities, not of individuals taken separately. Social facts are collective representations and ways of acting "capable of exercising over the individual an external constraint."[46] *The Rules of Sociological Method* prescribed that a sociologist must specify indicators of the social facts he wished to observe because only such external manifestations could be recorded, processed, and analyzed in research. The work of a sociologist could begin, then, only with a careful and self-conscious collection of social facts.[47]

Durkheim advised every sociologist to exclude all ideological prejudices or personal sentiments about observed phenomena so as to obtain an impartial scientific analysis quite external to the feelings that he might have. The sociologist was supposed to treat social phenomena of moral or immoral conduct purely as observational data, as things. In a similar way, he would distinguish carefully the conduct he wished to study from all sorts of mental states and attitudes that observed individuals might experience while showing such behavior. He would likewise distinguish moral conduct from the subjects' awareness of it or lack thereof and from their emotions or any other factors of individual psychology that could distort or refract or in any way influence observed behavior itself.

Observation was to be followed by (a) classification of social facts into a limited number of types, or social species, variously defined as morphological elements of population distribution or as crystallized social institutions (Chapters I, II. and IV); (b) definition of thus classified social facts as normal or pathological, i.e., as contributing or not contributing to social ends (Chapters II and III); (c) explanation of classified and defined social facts by accounting for their origins as antecedent causes and for their functions as effects or outcomes (Chapter V); and (d) comparative-experimental demonstration, or proof, of presented explanations using indicators as external manifestations of social facts (Chapter VI).

Following the ideal accepted in other experimental, and generally, empirical sciences of his time, Durkheim perceived Mill's inductive methods as fully applicable to sociology. Accordingly, his design for demonstrating the proof of social solidarity consisted in comparing the effects of common to uncommon, or unusual social conduct.[48] His explanation of mechanical and organic solidarity as two major functions of the division of labor was a direct product of this comparative "indirect-experimental" design based on the method of difference.[49] Durkheim referred to the method of difference and the method of concomitant variation and to induction in general as the new and proper method for sociology already in his early programmatic writings.[50] The only qualification he made for the use of the comparative-experimental method was that experiments in natural settings had to be replaced with indirect, i.e., quasi-experiments, for it was impossible to manipulate human social groups for scientific purposes. Durkheim also differentiated between historical and statistical comparisons. The former required qualitative, typological, and reconceptualizing studies, while the latter implied quantitative studies involving theory construction within already established or accepted conceptual systems.[51]

In *The Division of Labor*, morality associated with the most common social conduct was treated as absolutely necessary for sustaining collective human life over long historic periods of time, as its "indispensable minimum."[52] This inductive logic and comparative-experimental method remained standard tools in Durkheim's later work, especially in *The Elementary Forms*. In *Suicide*, Durkheim found that a classification of suicide did not add any new insight into the nature of this phenomenon interpreted as immoral.[53] Implicitly, however, he used in *Suicide* the same two morphological-structural types as in *The Division of Labor*: modern-Western as against ancient-primitive.

Until they re-emerged in *The Elementary Forms* as primitive religious beliefs and ritual practices, no explicit relation is to be found in Durkheim's earlier works between these two complementary elements of secular morality. The definition of normal social facts - as opposed to pathological – by their mere statistical preponderance led Durkheim to a paradoxical conclusion of the normality and usefulness of crime. Since crime is found in all societies and in all historic times, and since it can promote social change for the better – as vaccination is useful in developing immunity against certain diseases, – it must be normal and "healthy for society." These statements evoked sharp critical responses, notably from Tarde who disputed that normal could be defined as general.

The seemingly logical elegance of Durkheim's arguments did not convince Marxists either who rejected *The Rules* outright as "mysterious alchemy."[54] Indeed, it is questionable that crime can be seen as a social institution in the first place – rather than an outcome of criminalizing social practices. And if criminal law was an indicator of mechanical solidarity, crime as transgressions against such law could not be treated as a causal mechanism of modern social change either. Ironically, Durkheim himself made a similar distinction in "The Origins of Law" between law as an idea and as a set of statutes.[55] As he pointed out, the reviewed essay was about "the genesis not *of the law*, but *of the idea of the law*" (emphasis in the original). It showed, among other things, that parties in a conflict submit to the ruling of law primarily because it exists for them as an idea, or collective representation, of social solidarity, not by virtue of the authority or regulation of its rules.

Notes

[1] Durkheim (1893/1984, p. 130; 1902-1903/1961, pp. 5-14, 116-122). That led Durkheim to a critical position toward the explanation of Ancient Greek and Roman social institutions by religious beliefs in Fustel de Coulanges' *Ancient City*. The self-confident young sociologist accused his former teacher of mistaking cause for effect.

[2] Durkheim (1901/1983, pp. 122-128).

[3] Durkheim (1894/1982, pp. 11-24).

[4] See Durkheim (1885/1978, pp. 107, 114), Filloux (1977, pp. 20-21); cf. Jones (1994).

[5] Durkheim (1901/1983, pp. 24-31, 102-103, 120-129). The term social discipline was apparently derived from reviews of the German sociology of late 19th century (see 1885, p. 632; 1885/1978, p. 105; 1886, p. 68; 1897/1951, p. 251; 1901/1983, p. 128; 1902-1903/1961, pp. 17-46). Durkheim continued the theme of social discipline in subsequent works including *Suicide* and *Moral Education* (1886, p. 68; 1897/1951, p. 251; 1901/1983, p. 128; 1902-1903/1961, pp. 17-46).

[6] Durkheim (1902-1903/1961, pp. 29-31, 151-152).

[7] Durkheim (1894/1982, pp. 31-39). This is quoted verbatim and referred to hereafter accordingly to conform to existing translations. However, the French "*conscience collective*" in Durkheim does not translate into English simply as "collective consciousness" since it includes the meanings of both (cognitive) consciousness and (moral) conscience (see Parsons, 1937/1968, p. 309n3; Lukes, 1985, pp. 4-6).

[8] Durkheim (1894/1982, pp. 60, 68-72, 77-87).

[9] Durkheim (1893/1983).

[10] Durkheim (1893/1962, pp. 147-149, 153).

[11] Durkheim (1893/1984, p. 293).

[12] Durkheim (1893/1984, pp. 293-294).

[13] Durkheim, 1893/1984, p. 302).

[14] Durkheim (1893/1984, pp. 303-304).

[15] Durkheim (1893/1984, pp. 321-322).

[16] Durkheim (1897/1951, pp. 246-254, 259-276).

[17] Cf. Schoenfeld and Meštrović (1989).

[18] Durkheim (1902-1903/1961, pp. 82-83).

[19] Durkheim (1889/1978, pp. 115, 119, 255-256n18).
[20] Durkheim (1894/1982, p. 173).
[21] Durkheim (1894/1982, pp. 32, 118-123).
[22] Wallwork (1985).
[23] Pickering (1984, pp. 70-73).
[24] Durkheim (1903/1982, p. 200).
[25] Durkheim (1924/1953, p. 31).
[26] Durkheim (1898/1960, pp. 341-353).
[27] Durkheim (1955/1983, pp. 48-59, 110-112, 143-163).
[28] Durkheim (1924/1953, pp. 80-97).
[29] Durkheim (1924/1953, pp. 35-62).
[30] Pickering (1984, pp. 52-53, 78).
[31] Durkheim (1924/1953, pp. 169-212).
[32] Durkheim (1912/1965, pp. 13-21, 38, 51-63, 462-463).
[33] Durkheim (1912/1965, pp. 37-117).
[34] Durkheim (1914/1960, pp. 325-340), Pickering (1984, pp. 83-86).
[35] Durkheim (1912/1965, p. 467).
[36] Durkheim (1912/1965, pp. 236-245, 322-333, 475-479).
[37] Durkheim and Mauss (1963, p. 78).
[38] Durkheim (1912/1965, pp. 481-487; 1914/1960, p. 338; 1924/1953, p. 95; 1955/1983, pp. 103-105).
[39] Durkheim (1912/1965, p. 29; 1924/1953, pp. 18, 23-25, 30-32, 84).
[40] Durkheim (1912/1965, pp. 29-33, 169-172, 488-489; Durkheim and Mauss, 1963).
[41] Durkheim (1912/1965, pp. 474-479).
[42] Durkheim (1984, pp. xxxi-lix; 1898-1900/1983).
[43] Durkheim (1898/1960; 1900/1981; 1903/1982, pp. 175-210; 1905/1982, pp. 255-256; 1908a/1982, pp. 229-235; 1909/1978, pp. 78-82).
[44] Durkheim (1899/1982, pp. 120, 125).
[45] Durkheim (1900/1981; 1899/1982, pp. 241-244; 1909/1978, pp. 66-68, 79-80).
[46] Durkheim (1894/1982, pp. 38-47, 50-59; 1924/1953, pp. 49-52).
[47] Durkheim (1900/1981; 1903/1982, p. 69).
[48] Durkheim (1894/1982, pp. 87-97, 147-158).
[49] Durkheim (1894/1982, pp. 45, 57, 75, 123; 1893/1984, p. 11).
[50] Durkheim (1885/1978, pp. 95-96; 1887/1986-1987; 1888/1978a, pp. 47, 59; 1888/1978b, pp. 212, 223).
[51] Durkheim (1885/1978, p. 95; 1888/1978a, p. 62; 1888/1978b, pp. 209-210, 222; 1898/1960, pp. 342-343; 1905/1979; 1908/1982; 1909/1978, pp. 83, 86).
[52] Durkheim (1893/1984, p. 13).
[53] Durkheim (1897/1951, pp. 277-294)
[54] Lukes (1985, pp. 307-314).
[55] Durkheim (1893/1983, pp. 146-157).

6

Transition from Community to Society

Five years after completing his economic education, Talcott Parsons revolted against the utilitarianism, positivism, and empiricism in Anglo-American economic thought, including Alfred Marshall as its ultimate product, and set himself the task of establishing the science of sociology. He envisaged "a science which studies phenomena specifically social, those arising out of the interaction of human beings as such, which would hence not be reducible to the 'nature' of those human beings."[1] Parsons pronounced an indictment of atomistic individualism and empiricism against economics as a whole and formally proclaimed himself "a sociologist, not an economist." By contrast with economics studying the relationships of ends and means in subjective rational actions of informed atomized individuals, sociology would study normative rules and ultimate ends that members of society hold together in the form of organic value systems.[2] From that vantage point, Parsons offered a detached, sociological view of the neoclassic-institutionalist controversy in economics. In "Sociological

Elements in Economic Thought" Parsons gave a systematic critique of orthodox economic theories from a sociological position.[3] The work of Pareto, Durkheim, and Weber was presented as three different sociological ways of approaching traditional problems of economics in terms of social action. All these views were fully developed in *The Structure of Social Action* where Parsons outlined his idea of a voluntaristic mode of social action as opposed to prevailing ones.[4]

Structural-Functional Integration

Parsons distinguished between developmental processes of the social system as a whole and processes of functioning within it. Processes within the system are those of maintaining a "moving equilibrium" between instrumental motivation and normative value-orientations. This is achieved by social control. Parsons envisaged structural-functional analysis as the static aspect of his general sociology. Developmental changes of the social system were seen as comprised of unitary structural-functional phases in which social structures had a relative stability with respect to underlying processes of development as well as to its environment. Social functions provided a link between the static and the dynamic aspects of the system. They established functional relations within the system and between the system and its environment. Every social structure consists of patterns that "tend to be maintained" while social processes are the same patterns that "tend to develop." The functional significance of the social system is "inherently teleological" by which Parsons meant that a "process or set of conditions either 'contributes' to the maintenance or development of the system, or else it is 'dysfunctional' in that it detracts from the integration of the system."[5]

The dynamic aspect could also include causal explanations and predictions using quantitative techniques including mathematical models. Remarkably, Parsons' idea of causal analysis was not too far removed from statistical causal modeling. Writing half a century ago, Parsons occasionally sounded very much like today's causal model builders. "[The] essential feature of dynamic analysis in the fullest sense is the treatment of a body of *interdependent* phenomena simultaneously, in the mathematical sense. [...] The ideal solution is the possession of a logically complete system of dynamic generalizations which can state all the elements of reciprocal interdependence between all the variables of the system."[6] And more: "The essential question is how far the state of theory is developed to the point of permitting deductive transitions from one aspect or state of the system to another, so that it is possible to say that if the facts in A sector are W and X, those in B sector must be Y and Z."[7] Parsons did not believe that an adequate mathematical apparatus existed for such research procedures, but his initial program envisaged systems of simultaneous equations and tests of (functional) significance.[8] Apparently, he did not know that Sewell Wright had proposed the idea of path analysis already in the 1920's.[9]

In following his program of structural-functional analysis, Parsons defined its action frame of reference and its normative orientation to patterns of desirable standards of behavior. In *Toward a General Theory of Action*, Parsons and colleagues distinguished between "cathectic" orientation and value-orientation mediated by what he had previously called "ultimate values." In the context of collectivities the meaning of cathectically orientated action was similar to Simmel's "mass action" and Le Bon's "crowd" that later re-emerged in Chicago as (similarly unpredictable and irrational) "collective behavior." Parsons' value-orientation thus meant cathectic orientation subject to ideal normative principles, or standards.[10]

Interactions of a plurality of such units call for a "functional need of social integration." This provides focal points for the clustering of otherwise divergent and conflicting attitudes, symbols and action patterns. A social structure consists of patterned sectors of social roles played by actors relative to one another and of social statuses ranking people's achievement that can also be ascribed.[11] Roles are not merely "statistical trends," but properties of real actors having normative expectations from other actors. Such expectations form cultural traditions. Conformity or non-conformity with such traditions entails rewards or sanctions. Together with certain tolerances, the fulfillment of institutionalized social roles leads to the integration of "extremely varied potentialities of 'human nature'" thus guaranteeing the meeting of situational exigencies of society and of its members.[12]

Institutions themselves are also functionally differentiated and organized by types of roles. There are "situational" or "expressive" institutions such as kinship, political, or cultural, but also "instrumental" ones such as professions. Social stratification organizes all social roles by institutions of the former or the latter kind. Since institutions form a functionally differentiated structure, it is possible "to place changes in any one part of it" and follow the repercussions of such changes for other elements of the entire social structure. Institutional roles are never perfectly integrated, however.[13] Social statuses and social roles form a bundle called status-roles that "are not generally an attribute of the actor, but are units of the social system."[14] The integration of these bundles of differentiated and stratified social roles and statuses as the "foci of crystallization for social structure" involves their coordinated organization. A solution of this problem is tantamount to the solution of the Hobbesian problem of order.[15]

Confronted with the facts of growing fascist movements in Europe, Parsons offered his early analysis of the process of social change. He conceived it as strains and conflicts in social structure resulting in a breakdown of social integration despite the fact that this breakdown involved both privileged elites and popular masses. Parsons compared the fascist movements to revolutionary and religious ones that disrupted a smooth functioning of the social system. Fascist nationalism was "the lowest common denominator of traditionalistic sentiments," but above all, these movements involved institutionalized vested interests and privileges of certain status groups such as landed nobility and clergy in Spain and the Junker class in Germany. These groups could exercise influence on power relations "through channels other than those open to the masses, through political intrigue, financial influence, and so on," so that they could more easily disrupt traditional social order in defense of their interests. At the same time, fascism claimed traditional cultural and political values which threatened the interest of new business elites.[16]

Parsons specified cultural tradition as consisting of externalized value-orientations. As standards of institutional role-expectations, they guarantee the fulfillment of actors' moral obligations to a collectivity and to society at large. To the extent that such values are shared and become common, individual actors manifest patterns of conforming social conduct despite their self-interest and instrumental goal-orientations. This is how a social system of any scale becomes integrated. Even the American business firm restricts its instrumental production goals of maximizing profits by certain technical standards.[17] This cultural system is supplemented by the social and the personality subsystems, the latter being crucial for the study of socialization in its function of securing conformity with normative standards in adult life. Modern social order is maintained by each one of these institutional subsystems relying on the other two.[18]

Interpenetration of Pattern-Variables

Parsons found that the roles of adult male businessmen, professionals, and administrative officials could be characterized as universalistic within the limits of their specific occupational, jurisdictional, etc., domains. By contrast, the roles of business customers, professional clients, administrative subordinates, and young people and women in general were characterized as particularistic and functionally diffuse.[19] Parsons associated this difference with the ways of status attainment. Businessmen, professionals, and officials achieved their status in occupations, whereas women, young and old people, customers, clients, and subordinates had it ascribed to them on the basis of membership in a kinship group or personal qualities such as age, sex, beauty, intelligence, and strength.[20]

The seeds of non-conformity and of frustrated role-expectations are found in the difference between socialization having to do with value-orientations, and learning that relies on imitation. This conflict begins with the differentiation of a child's attitudes into diffuse and specific ones. Next comes the differentiation, along the same lines of socialization and learning, of expressive and instrumental priorities, often allocated along feminine-masculine lines. At a still later point in life, this polarization acquires the form of particularism and universalism. Finally, socialization and learning produce the opposition of ascriptive and achievement (or quality-performance) orientations.[21] Instrumental and expressive orientations became a particular focus of Parsons' concept of a functioning social system facilitating the integration of highly differentiated status-roles. This interpenetration of *Gemeinschaft* and *Gesellschaft* type orientations provides a solution to the main problem of a normally functioning social system, that of allocating roles among actors and their status groups.[22]

In *The Social System,* Parsons began cross-classifying these categories - now called pattern-variables - with a view of methodically obtaining four-cell tables of typical theoretical concepts that could be used in empirical descriptions and classifications while also being meaningful as general sociological categories at the same time. Inevitably, the complexity of these multi-level cross-classifications was growing with every page. Parsons did not have special succinct categories for the contents of these recurring four cells, and that created a problem. This semantic difficulty was even more pronounced in Parsons' attempts at cross-classifying all the pairs of pattern-variables in Chapter III of *The Social System* where *Gemeinschaft-* and *Gesellschaft*-type orientations were also combined in "permutations" within these same categories. While empirical illustrations of these cross-classifications clearly implied interpenetration of *Gemeinschaft-* and *Gesellschaft*-type notions, the lack of special, semantically cogent categories describing them entangled Parsons' endeavor to develop a conceptual framework in an increasingly verbose analytical discourse of never diminishing abstractness. Parsons found a solution in the concept of boundary zones.

In situations of social interaction among adults as, for example, between a physician and his patient, diffuse and particularistic orientations often collide with specific and universalistic ones. A doctor enters an interactive situation with a prospective patient with strong achievement, universalistic, affectively-neutral, and functionally-specific orientations. By contrast, the patient comes with strong ascriptive, particularistic, affective, and diffuse orientations toward the physician's role-performance. In a successful interaction, they both transfer and countertransfer their initial orientations to each other. Some of the "transferrings" from the patient are institutionalized in the form of negative disciplinary sanctions accepted by the medical profession, like prohibition to advertise, to bargain with the patient for fees, and to refuse to treat "poor credit risks." The patient expects the physician to know that he "deals with human beings." In turn, the physician tries to make his patient realize that the warm and friendly attitude must be underemphasized in the interest of patient's own welfare. Situations of medical practice end up controlled by a combination of both types of pattern-variables.[23] Since both professionals and business people were involved in the same *Gesellschaft*-type roles, i.e., universalistic, affectively-neutral, specific and achievement-oriented, the only difference Parsons found between them was in self- vs. collectivity-orientation. With the elimination of the self-collectivity pattern-variable by 1953, this difference was all but lost for Parsons' conceptual scheme.

In *Family, Socialization and Interaction Process* published after World War II, Parsons and Bales noted a larger participation of American women in the labor force. While still enjoying the ascription of the husband's higher status, woman now also had a "boundary role" of her own where the external (*Gesellschaft*) occupational roles and the internal (*Gemeinschaft*) family roles interpenetrated.[24] In Chapter 3 of *The Working Papers* Bales' twelve categories of social-emotional problems arising in task-oriented small groups were reduced to six symmetrical positive and negative pairs and then to four. Parsons associated each of the four interaction problems - Adaptive, Instrumental, Expressive, and Integrative - with a pair of pattern-variables as "different ways of conceptualizing the same thing."[25] In Chapter 5, the names of the two middle categories, Instrumental and Expressive, were changed to Goal-gratifying and Latent, respectively. Then Bales' categories were interpreted dynamically, as phases in a change of system state, i.e., in its functioning, and a necessary change was made in the associations of Parsons' pattern-variables with Bales' newly-renamed categories. In this way, pure *Gemeinschaft* and *Gesellschaft* orientations were subsumed under Adaptation and Integration, and their interpenetrations under Goal-gratification and Latent tension-management as paradigmatic social functions, essentially, as functional imperatives. This is how the AGIL four-function paradigm was born.

Societal Exchange and Value Standards

The idea of two boundary zones as the locus of the interpenetration of Adaptation and Integration became central in *Economy and Society*. However, its meaning was changed. While the family study of a year before considered dual boundary zones between selected pairs of functional subsystems, *Economy and Society* co-authored with Smelser and all later works - where the interchange model was used - changed the meaning of interpenetration from mutual bilateral mediation of polar opposites to a multilateral, all-to-all process.[26] In *Economy and Society* Parsons offered his conception of modern impersonal economic exchange relations. After circumscribing the boundaries and the internal structure of the economic subject-matter, he discussed elements of its structure, followed by their functioning, and finally, its growth. Many of central economic categories do come in fours, notably four factors of production - capital, labor, entrepreneurship, and land; and four major economic functions – production, consumption, allocation, and exchange. Parsons offered a bold interpretation of these and many other economic concepts in terms of Adaptation,

Goal-gratification, Integration, and Latent pattern-maintenance functional requisites that he declared to be universal to all social systems and their subsystems. Economy as a whole was associated with Adaptation, while Goal-attainment was assigned to polity. The I- and L-functions were assigned - some time later - to "fiduciary culture"[27] and "societal community," respectively.[28]

Economic subsystems were obtained from a further specification of the Adaptation function of the total social system. Thus four second-level economic processes and factors were obtained: (A_A) capitalization, or capital; (A_G) production, distribution, and sale, or labor; (A_I) entrepreneurship; and (A_L) economic commitments, or land.[29] Using the same iterative technique, these were further broken down into a total of sixteen functional economic subprocesses, or subsystems.[30] The functioning of this economic system consisted of two-way interchanges of all functional processes, or factors, with all others of their proper levels. For example, (A_A) investment and (G_A) political encouragement of economic activity were interpreted as two boundary zones of the interchange and interpenetration between (A) economy and (G) polity. During such an interchange a total of six possible input-output pairs of mediating boundary zones were discovered within each of the sixteen functional foursomes, and numerous others suggested for their external boundaries containing many familiar economic notions. For example, wages and consumer goods-and-services as outputs of production are exchanged for labor services and consumer spending that are the outputs of household and production's inputs. This is nothing but an interchange between two kinds of second-level Goal-attainment within the total social system, namely, between (A_G) Goal-attainment of Adaptation and (L_G) Goal-attainment of Latent pattern-maintenance.

Likewise, when the right of government to intervene in economic activity and its control of productivity are exchanged, as the outputs of the economic system, for control over capital funds and the encouragement of productive enterprise, as the outputs of the political system and economy's inputs, this means

an interchange between two functional subprocesses of Adaptation: between (A_A) Adaptation of Adaptation, and (G_A) Adaptation of Goal-attainment. The duality of inputs and outputs is related to the intervening role of money as the medium that facili-
tates exchanges within specialized subsystem boundaries, e.g., of
factors of production in economy. The same takes place in exchanges across those boundaries since producers of other specialized goods or services, e.g., politicians, also consume economic
goods and services produced outside of their functional subsystem. The duality of social interchange is also reflected in the dual
nature of money. Money "represents the generalization of the
purchasing power to control decisions to exchange goods; on the
other hand it symbolizes attitudes. [...] If it cannot command
goods and services money is not acceptable as wages; if it cannot
symbolize prestige and mediate between detailed symbols and a
broader symbolization it is not acceptable on other grounds.
Only with this dual significance can money perform is social
functions".[31]

A good economic system is a stable one, that maintains a
balance, or equilibrium, in all innumerable instances of social interchange, i.e., between all inputs and all outputs of various economic and non-economic functional subsystems. Instability of
socio-economic interchange may lead either to a restoration of
equilibrium or to its further amplification. The latter is also a major causative factor of economic growth and institutional structural change. Economic change was conceived as a "middle
ground," or combination of intra- and inter-institutional social
structural shifts. Thus the historic separation of property ownership and control of business resulted in changes for American
social stratification. Career managers wrestled real control of large
corporations from "great industrial magnates and their families"
without this resulting in a revolution even while the ruling capitalist class was subjected to progressive taxation.

Parsons criticized Schumpeter for his prediction of the
inevitability of socialism replacing capitalism and suggested "a
third possibility." He presented the traditional socioeconomic

system of classical capitalism as an outcome of a similar differentiation of feudal kinship into ownership and control. The two institutional domains acquired the names "economic" and "political." Modernization meant a further differentiation of these two domains. Hence the parallel processes of bureaucratization and democratization which means that the evolving modern social system is neither capitalism nor socialism, but something inbetween. From this Parsons concluded that economic measurement needed "some other standard - to which money values and costs are themselves relative."[32]

In *Theories of Society*, Parsons drew a parallel between money and power as circulating media controlling the allocation of economic and political resources respectively, and also as scarce resources in their own right.[33] This idea was further developed in his papers on the place of force, and on the concepts of power, influence, and value-commitment.[34] All were treated as circulating media of interchange similar to money. Thus, speaking of socially shared value-commitments, Parsons noted that their stock is always limited, and that problems arise from the nonobservance of a judicial balance between giving and implementing them. Constituents contribute political support to common assets of the "power-bank" that are then spent, or liquidated by public office-holders during their implementation. Political commitments are exchanged "through giving and withdrawing support for various collective goals." They can be implemented "on demand" or deferred, and they can be inflated or deflated.

A social unit may be "overcommitted" when it has too many, too diverse, and too serious commitments to be implemented effectively. Overcommitment leads to moral inflation. The opposite phenomenon, that of "moral deflation," is manifested in the unwillingness on the part of a social unit to honor commitments already made. McCarthyism was a case of a political deflation in the USA.[35] Parsons went on to spread the interchange model to the cultural and the personality systems, finding additional media of cultural and personality interchange. Eventually, he introduced "behavioral organism" as the fourth system complementing society, personality, and culture, and designated intelligence, performance-capacity, affect, and definition of the situation as the four media for this most general level of his frame of reference.[36]

The Eroding Meanings of AGIL Categories

Parsons conceived the AGIL categories as four paradigmatic social functions, but also as phases of a dynamic procedure of social functioning. While he postulated that none of the AGIL elements could be reduced to any other as orthogonal dimensions of a four-dimensional Euclidian space,[37] he distinguished between their earlier and later functional phase movements, and spoke about their (recursive) sequence in the direction of motivational energy flow toward Goal-attainment. Parsons also spoke of the reverse (non-recursive) symbolic-controlling movement from Goal-attainment to Latent pattern-management, for example, in performance and learning. In the evolutionary scheme the energizing strength came from Adaptation while the controlling strength came from Latent pattern-maintenance.[38] What then was wrong with the AGIL paradigm? While helping to make his conceptualizations less verbose and more readable, this reorganization of Parsons' analytical apparatus did not come without a price.

The AGIL four-function paradigm organized Parsons' conceptual apparatus, but it also added new complications to his thought. Bales' concepts on which AGIL categories were based commanded their own meanings that implied certain usages and precluded certain others. This raised a problem of justifying the identification of combinations of pattern-variables with particular AGIL categories. Parsons also had to demonstrate that these combinations were consistent with Bales' understanding of process as a linear succession of phases each related only to its preceding and succeeding ones. Parsons began speaking about process as intermittent, but also as circular and spiral. He was flexible and shrewd in making a disclaimer that the AGIL sequence of the four functions was provisional only, that it had been obtained as a "certain generalization" from Bales' empirical research in small-group dynamics, and that besides a simple reversal, "other phase [sequences are] possible." Moreover, the names of the four functional phases were also incidental, literally appropriate only to face-to-face interaction in small groups.[39]

However, the AGIL formula triggered a virtual avalanche of new conceptual formulations, and in the process all Parsons' previous caveats were soon forgotten. In particular, why did Parsons place the Integration phase that accommodated all pure *Gemeinschaft* orientations in the middle position rather than in the end of the process where it properly belonged? One obvious reason was that despite writing about a process, Parsons was still depicting his new model graphically in the same 2x2 crosstabulation table. With all the changes of focus and terminology, the sequential order of the third and fourth phases in Bales' original functional problems, detailed on pages 64, 74, and 79 (Chapter 3), became reversed on page 180. It was apparently an oversight. In any event, the erroneous AGIL order of functional phases was accepted "as a handy idealized model," and in this form it entered into all Parsons' conceptualizations and theories that followed - rather than the more correct one - AGLI. This hardly noticeable error of order compounded even more the inconsistencies of Parsons' subsequent work. The enormous remedial effort Parsons spent during the 1960's and the 1970's to reconcile those inconsistencies can in part be traced to this small error.

The cybernetic idea of two-way hierarchies of natural conditions and artificial controls, that Parsons first used in "An Approach to Psychological Theory"[40] amplified and further developed his earlier characterization of the system processes in the AGIL four-function paradigm as directed from motivational energy to symbolic control and back. The difference between the polar *Gemeinschaft* and *Gesellschaft*-type orientations in all the four pattern-variables became quickly obscured by the new crosscutting distinction between motivational, actor-related pattern-variables, on the one hand, and situational, object-related ones, on the other. This loss of connection with the pattern-variables and, therefore, with the social action content in AGIL already happened in *Economy and Society* - notwithstanding the "Technical Note" to the contrary,[41] and except for one revisit[42] it soon became all but history.

The third modification of the AGIL scheme came in "Some Problems of General Theory in Sociology" where Parsons subsumed the AGIL functional categories under two crosscutting dimensions, or axes: action space and time, both understood naturalistically, as those of "any living system."[43] Adaptation was now characterized as external instrumental, Goal-attainment as external consummatory, Integration as internal consummatory, and Latency as internal instrumental. This idea was present already in "Pattern-Variables Revisited," but there it was obscured by the complicating cross-classification of all the four system phases themselves.[44] Now two of the four "general systemic" functions were clearly internal, i.e., directly relevant to any system within the same level of analysis, and only two had any temporal order.

Notes

[1] Parsons (1932, p. 338).

[2] Parsons (1934a).

[3] Parsons (1934b; 1935).

[4] Parsons (1937/1968). Beside Pareto, Durkheim, and Weber, Parsons also recognized Marx and Engels as standing "in an important line of the development of social science rather than only as the ideological founders of 'scientific socialism' […]". While pointing out the importance of conflicting class interests in any social analysis, he noted the utopianism of the idea of a classless society (1945/1954a, pp. 228-230).

[5] Parsons (1945/1954a, pp. 214-218; 1951 pp. 480-483).

[6] Parsons (1945/1954a, pp. 215-216. Emphasis in the original).

[7] Parsons (1951, p. 21).

[8] Parsons (1945/1954a, pp. 215-218; 1951, pp. 21-22).

[9] See Blalock (1971, Part II).

[10] Parsons (1935/1991); Parsons et al (1951, pp. 4-6), Tolman (1951, pp. 343-346).

[11] Parsons (1940/1954b, pp. 69-78; 1951 pp. 26-35). Social rankings can also be in the form of class by which Parsons meant kinship groups of equal status. In that sense, Parsons (1945/1954a, pp. 228-230) believed that "Class conflict certainly exists in the

United States, but it is different from the German case [...] The Marxian theory of class conflict [is] a step in the development of a social science [...]." While noting the importance of occupational, leadership, and property divisions, Parsons observed that highly differentiated American social stratification was much more complex than that presented by Marx. Observing the important integrating function of the kinship system, Parsons concluded that American class was identical with family status (1949/1954).

[12] Parsons (1945/1954a, p. 231).

[13] Parsons (1945/1954b, p. 232, 240; 1951, pp. 51-53).

[14] Parsons (1951, pp. 25-26, 36-57; 1953/1954, pp. 388-389).

[15] Parsons (1951, pp. 113-136).

[16] Parsons (1942/1954a, pp. 124-125, 138-140).

[17] Parsons (1951, pp. 36-42, 53; 1953/1954, p. 388).

[18] Parsons (1945/1954a; 1950/1954).

[19] Parsons (1939/1954; 1942/1954a).

[20] Parsons (1940/1954a; 1940/1954b, pp. 79-80, 86-88; 1942/1954a; 1943/1954, pp. 190-196). Yet in his analysis of the social structure of pre-Nazi Germany, Parsons used class rather than status categories - army officers, landed Prussian Junker aristocracy, civilian administrative bureaucracy, members of liberal professions, bourgeoisie, elected officials representing special interests, industrial workers, peasants, and housewives (1942/1954b).

[21] Parsons (1951, pp. 63-66, 81-83, 88-96, 154-161, 216-242, 280-281; Parsons and Bales, 1955, pp. 45-47, 123-131, 134-135).

[22] Parsons (1951, pp. 113-150; 1952, pp. 190-233).

[23] Parsons (1942/1954b; 1951, pp. 433-435, 438, 454, 460-462).

[24] Parsons and Bales (1955, p. 13).

[25] Parsons, Bales and Shils (1953).

[26] Parsons and Smelser (1956).

[27] Parsons (1960/1967, pp. 8-28). Fiduciary culture was distinguished from diachronic Culture in the anthropological sense, on par with Personality and the Social system.

[28] Parsons (1966).

[29] Four years later, in "Some Principal Characteristics of Industrial Societies" (1960), Parsons replaced entrepreneurship with organization. The latter was understood as business administration, the most recent functionally differentiated economic factor that Parsons also brought up earlier, in "Some Reflections on the Institutional Framework of Economic Development" (1958/1960b).

[30] Parsons and Smelser (1956, pp. 196-218).

[31] Parsons and Smelser (1956, pp. 70-78, 139-143).

[32] Parsons and Smelser (1956, pp. 30, 246-294).

[33] Parsons (1961b).

[34] Parsons (1964/1967a, 1963/1967a, 1963/1967b, 1968/1969).

[35] Parsons (1963/1967a, pp. 308-309, 313-314, 317, 331, 337-343; 1964/1967a, pp. 290-291; 1968/1969, pp. 457-458, 464).

[36] Parsons (1975/1977; Parsons and Platt, 1973, pp. 304-305n2)

[37] Parsons, Bales, and Shils (1953, pp. 63-109).

[38] Parsons (1966, pp. 16-19).

[39] Parsons, Bales, and Shils (1953, pp. 72, 172, 179, 188, 193).

[40] Parsons (1959a).
[41] Parsons and Smelser (1956, pp. 33-38).
[42] Parsons (1960/1967).
[43] Parsons (1970/1977a).
[44] Parsons (1960/1967).

7

Achievements of Social Historicism

While the basic principles of Marx's materialist philosophy of history have been slowly gaining followers in Western historiographic thought since Marx's time, their applied theoretical and practical realizations have been continuously questioned in both communist and anti-communist literature, and Marx's own concrete predictions proved mostly wrong or irrelevant. On the contrary, his youthful manuscripts on humanistic communism published much later have been widely hailed. They were seen as representing an essential element of our humanity, as something that the communist movement was too hasty to throw out for the sake of an all-out communist revolution centered exclusively on institutional, primarily, economic issues. The communist movement itself inspired by Marx's work has experienced persistent opposition, both internal - in such revisionist figures as Bernstein, Lukács, and Korsch - and external.[1]

Economics was the only established social science in Marx's time, and these class interests were described as economic ones. For today's highly developed societies this is a very limited if fundamental way of characterizing material interests. Hence all the critiques of Marxist economic reductionism as well as determinism. Cultural and political interests can be as much material as economic ones - as Bourdieu demonstrated. What we know as culture, technology, and social order itself are basically human artifacts promising a chance of prolonging natural time and extending natural space by intensifying them.

Social Justice

Marx's *Capital* is a combination of positive theory of capitalist economy and fragments of a critical analysis of classical economics found throughout its three volumes. The "ascent to the concrete" of *Capital* was preceded by a comprehensive critical "descent to the abstract" of the *Grundrisse* completed about 1859. It was followed by a presentist history of the economic science in *Theories of Surplus-Value* planned as Volume Four of *Capital*.[2] *Theories of Surplus-Value* can be said to be a critique in yet another sense – that of giving an alternative interpretation of the capitalist mode of production by exegetically reading an external reality of surplus-value into the classical authors, rather than giving their immanent critique, a critique on their own merits.

The main message of Marx's *Capital* was that the whole system of capitalist economic relations was fundamentally unfair, defective, and therefore unsustainable. Capitalist relations of production were constantly undermined as were relations of social exchange and social distribution. The proportions between and within their determining production of the means of production and production of the means of consumption that were necessary for maintaining an equilibrium of the entire system of economic relations were never observed under capitalism - whether it was simple or expanded reproduction.

Marx's concept of exploitation of one class by another was based on the idea of surplus-value as a measure of unfair exchange of inputs and outputs of production and unfair distribution of incomes in the form of workers' wages and capitalists' profits. That explained the grossly unfair social distribution of living conditions between these two classes. The idea of surplus-value implied a greater value of workers' labor power than was reflected in its monetary compensation, i.e., social injustice. Marx did ridicule contemporary notions of justice dismissing them as part of deceptive and self-serving bourgeois ideology. But this was said referring only to the legalistic justice of private property relations - rather than the unfair class relations that indicated the unsustainability of the entire capitalist social system.

When Marx set out to critique modes of production he did so when the classic economic science still adhered to the labor theory of value where economic value was inextricably tied to cost of production. He saw the working class as involved in production – as opposed to the unproductive classes of capitalists and merchants. World history was presented as a change of inequitable modes of production – slavery, feudalism, capitalism. And yet, Marx's focus was not industrial production per se even when he spoke about the intensification of labor. Rather it was unfair exchange of the benefits that the two antagonistic classes derived from their relationship – wages and profits. It was all about unfair exchange of divergent class interests. Modes of production in that sense turns out to be a misleading term as soon as one brings up the difference between conflicting class interests in what Marx called production relations. It was all about modes of social distribution and social exchange. In at least one spot in *Grundrisse*, Marx in fact mentioned exchange between classes.[3]

Where Marx and Engels spoke of observed dismal living conditions of the working class, Weber who was involved in rigorous empirical research of such conditions in Germany spoke of them in probabilistic terms as life chances and associated them with achieved or else inherited social status. While he duly noted social imparities in the distribution of life chances, Weber never explicitly associated them with the idea of social justice even if that very idea – that he found in Ancient Judaism - was at the core of his life-long studies of value-rationality and of the historic process of rationalization itself. Despite the fact that a "shadow of exploitation" can be found in Weber's writings,[4] Weber was much more concerned with the individualistic legal form of justice in the process of rationalization rather than with the fundamental idea of justice in exchange between classes lying at its foundation, both substantively and historically. While both Marx and Weber implicitly addressed the problem of historic social justice, for Marx it was a matter of future-oriented social progress, for Weber it was a matter of origin in a distant past of Western social order.

Marx justified his prediction of a communist revolution initially by his deterministic philosophical conception of history as driven by class struggle and then substantiated by a social-scientific unsustainability analysis in *Capital*. Weber, on the other hand, implied a probabilistic and indeterminate "adequate causation" in any process of historic development intimately fused with "chance causation." The latter could include voluntaristic social action as well as natural or other accidental factors.

Besides trying to offer a conception of social classes that would be an alternative to Marx's idea of class struggle as responsible for historic social change, Weber highlighted his concept of status groups as similarly stratified groupings across various institutional domains and defined by social rank based on honor. This stress on status and status groups was also supported by Weber's historicist if indeterminate outlook to the past. Weber's early work in economic history followed Marx's concept of class rather closely, but in his later draft fragment on status and class in *Economy and Society* class and status are seen as overlapping.

Status and Class Connection

Weber's idea of status and status groups, and Marx's notion of social classes can be seen as two separate yet complementary ways of addressing the problem of social stratification, social justice, and social action. For any social movement to be effective, and have an inspiring substantive message, it must reflect certain essential interests or be opposed to some others. The most essential social interests that have always been pursued in human history are material ones, those having to do with the (usually unfair) distribution of limited objectified social space and social time. Settlement and property classes are objectified forms of stratified extensive and intensive social space, just as industry and political classes are objectified forms of stratified extensive and intensive social time.[5]

From this point of view, distributive social justice and justice in exchange involve a relationship of mutual dependence between structures of status groups and of their class interests. Within the framework of such an analysis, social classes represent special interests in the sphere of exchange whereas status groups stand for stratified social distribution of family, educational, or other life chances. As it was for Weber, status differences can be registered by social scientists interested in observing and summarizing social distributions of living conditions. Differences of class, however, are social realities that affect prevailing impersonal, more removed relationships of status groups' shared interests where the need for social action to change class relations may be less obvious and by the same token more crucial. If unfair distributions of achieved social status are subject to public opinion and social action, an obsolescent, inequitable class structure usually involves heightened class consciousness leading to status groups taking action, a stand either to promote and defend their shared class interests or downgrade certain others. If a social movement is to be successful and historical, all such class interests must be gauged correctly – as objective possibilities in Weber's sense.

Weber treated and presented orientation of social action as ideal-typical values involved in the historical understanding of social conduct and thus, as a primary subject-matter of any causal explanation of institutional social order. Here also belongs his notion of vocation as a commitment to pursue such values. Hence Weber's idea of *Lebensfuhrung* as a dedicated, methodical conduct of life. Despite his terminology of social action in comparative macro-social studies however, Weber's value-rational orientations have more to do institutional behavior than with status groups' self-conscious class action. Any status group can be differentiated by class, and all class interests can be differentiated by status groups that share them as well as by their institutional domains.

As a matter of fact, the differentiation of class interests by high, medium, or low social status was the original meaning of social stratification in Marxist literature, especially in the revisionist writings, such as those of Eduard Bernstein. The opposite also happens to be true. The idea of social class was born long before Marx when it meant power and wealth differentiation among European aristocracy, clergy, and the military whose members enjoyed equally high status honor. This orthogonal relationship between classes and status groups is one reason why they have been often confused or used interchangeably in American literature since Lloyd Warner.[6] Yet class is not defined by the kind of a car you drive or by the kind of neighborhood you live in. These are differences of status and they may be used to define status groups. Unlike achieved or inherited status that is a matter of prestige and honor and that is meant to be visible, even conspicuous, class is defined by our position in the much less ostentatious structures of wealth and power relations.[7]

It is these structures of deep-seated class interests that are the big secrets hiding behind misleading ideologies that social scientists have always tried to debunk. The concept of classes as real groups was justifiably rejected during the 20th-century ideological struggle against the militant Communist International in several of its emanations, especially against its totalitarian Marxism of the Soviet variety. It was therefore argued that classes do not exist in advanced Western societies, particularly not in the USA with its democratic traditions. But democracy and representative government do not in the least preclude the existence of status groups and their class interests.

Conflicts of class interests do not necessarily have to be in the form of storming the Bastille as in Paris or storming the Winter Palace as in St. Petersburg. They can move from the street to parliamentary institutions, to TV screens, and now to You-Tube, Facebook, and Twitter. Habermas (1984, 1987) captured this transition in his concept of communicative action. Only he modeled it - in his notion of the public sphere - on intimate café settings where members of educated cultural elites could debate prevailing polarized ideologies. To be effective, communicative class struggle needs something better - a substantive language of fair exchange among upper, middle, and lower classes as well as of distributive social justice among high, medium, and low status groups. Lacking such a language, the U.S. Congress turns into a forum for ritualized debates among representatives of the two catch-all political parties who are supported by lobbyists' money and try to reconcile the special interests of corporations, industries and states - rather than a public space where stratified status groups can peacefully resolve their differences of class interests.[8]

Typology of Social Classes

At first glance, the differences between Marx and Weber are glaring: the effect of material forces on historic development vs. the role of religious values; the historic role of social classes vs. prestige-seeking status groups; revolutionary working class movement vs. individual social action; a devastating critique of capitalist social order and promotion of a proletarian revolution vs. a mild critique of unforeseen outcomes of rationalization; revolutionary class consciousness and class action vs. rationality in the orientation of mundane social conduct; militant secularism vs. religion as the locus of high moral values. Marxists have invariably referred to Weber's social analysis as "bourgeois sociology." In contrast to class and class struggle that were at the center of Marxist thought, Weber's work presented social stratification as centered primarily on the idea of social status and status groups differing in the degree of honor and prestige either inherited or achieved. But this is so only if we limit our reading Weber to his unfinished definitional fragments on status, class, and party. Actually, Weber must be seen as a major seminal source on the formation of all major social class types.

Marx left an impressive analysis of the historic origins of economic (property) classes and of their mid-19th century social structure identifying the deeply antagonistic relationship between the upper class of capitalists and the lower class of impoverished industrial proletariat. The existence of certain European middle classes was also pointed out, notably in *Eighteenth Brumaire*. While Marx described the formation of economic classes in the differential historic process of capital accumulation, Weber gave a more detailed conception of the process of Western rationalization. But what is rationalization in Weber's sense? It is much more than the process of certain ascetic sects acquiring value-rational orientations leading to a meaningful methodical conduct of life. That was only the starting point in the Protestant ethic. Further development of Western rationalization took the form of the historic processes of bureaucratization and professionalization as its two major ingredients. If we add the historic process of urbanization also vividly described by Weber, we will find that his historic writings lend themselves to an interpretation as processes of class formation

The three types of (taxonomic) social classes whose formation can be deduced from Weber's historic writings - even if they do not conform to Weber's own explicit notion of social class – are settlement, industry, and political. It is in and by the processes of differential urbanization, industrialization, and bureaucratization that these distinct types of social classes have been forming historically. The term political classes is preferred here to bureaucratic to avoid the derogatory connotation of inefficiency and red tape associated with bureaucracy in today's popular usage. The categories of industry classes coincide with broad industry sectors where in today's post-industrial society we also list professional and support services in addition to manual workers in farming and manufacturing. With professionals as the upper industry class, we can thus account for industry class formation as the modern outcome of differential industrialization and professionalization processes.

In the absence of the concepts of status groups, Marx conceived of the social divisions of his time in terms of property classes. The term petty-bourgeoisie is widely used in Marxist literature as representing groups of medium economic class while the term big bourgeoisie is used synonymously with the class of capitalists, i.e., big property owners. The original etymological meaning of bourgeoisie is simply European town-dwellers as opposed to peasantry settled in open rural areas and aristocrats protected in their castles. Today we must also speak of suburbanites and residents of large metropolitan centers as two additional categories of settlement classes formed in the historic process of urbanization and suburbanization.

Weber could not have given names to all these classes that are specific to the empirical social realities of our time. This fact may even be propitious for sociology. Marx's concept of property classes was appropriate for his time and place. As a consequence, there is still a lack of analytical distinction between settlement, industry, economic, and political classes in sociological literature. Marx's capitalists – big property owners - were also industrialists, business executives, and power holders. While work in industries separated from residential settlement earlier in history, property ownership separated from administration only in the 20th century.[9] Not having from Weber any explicit class taxonomy designated for settlement, economic, industry or political classes leaves us free and unencumbered by dated or undifferentiated concepts to form our own conceptual scheme for four major types of social classes whose formation was explored by Weber.

Notes

[1] Bottomore (1975, pp. 19-20) noted that Eduard Bernstein's early revisionism did not go far enough in its effort to translate Marxism into the language of sociology. Indeed, it did not touch the heart of Marx's historical materialism – the relationship between the historic progress of means of production and production relations.

[2] Marx (1971).

[3] Marx (1857-1858/1973, p. 108).

[4] Wright (2002).

[5] Smikun (2005).

[6] Not so in the European literature. See Chan and Goldthorpe (2004, 2007).

[7] Veblen's critique of "conspicuous consumption" was based on these distinctive characteristics of "the leisure class" showing off its high status rather than its source.

[8] Vanneman and Cannon (1987) convincingly argued that the absence of classic militant forms of class struggle in the United States does not in the least mean the absence of social classes.

[9] Berle and Means (1932).

8

The Relevance of Functionalism

It was owing to Durkheim's and his followers' relentless work that sociology became a movement in French academic circles, and eventually, an established, legitimate discipline in university curricula. Yet sociology owes its modest but secure place on the map of social sciences mainly to Parsons' untiring efforts at building a general sociological theory from its several earlier versions. Owing in large measure to translations and interpretations by Talcott Parsons, the categories of social action and its orientations, goal- and value-rationality, disenchantment and rationalization, charisma and bureaucracy, historical individuals and ideal types, judgments of fact and value judgments are an integral part of the common language used by social scientists the world over. Like no one else before him, Parsons advanced the status of sociology as a science and elevated its general theory – or conceptual schemes - to an unprecedented height.

 Durkheim explored the functions of the division of labor as a transition from mechanical to organic social solidarity, from repressive law to restitutional law, from society as a collection of individuals following authoritarian rules to one as a self-regulating body of autonomous groups adjusting their particular interest to the common good of all social groups. Parsons' structural-functional approach to the analysis of social systems similarly bracketed their evolution from community to modern society – from *Gemeinschaft* to *Gesellschaft*. That was in spite of the long fragment on Tönnies' *Gemeinschaft und Gesellschaft* appended to Part III of *The Structure of Social Action* devoted to Weber. Parsons concluded his analysis of Tönnies with a warning that also sounded like a program of future work. "But this discussion of *Gemeinschaft* and *Gesellschaft* should not be taken to mean that these categories are unreservedly acceptable as the basis for a general classification of social relationships or, indeed, that it is possible to reduce to start from any dichotomy of only two types. [...] To attempt to develop such a scheme of classification would be definitely outside the scope of the present study."[1]

Parsons saw Tönnies' contrast of traditional community and modern society paralleled in Marx's theme of a transition from primitive communism to modern capitalism, in Durkheim's theme of the transition from mechanical to organic solidarity, and in Weber's theme of Western rationalization of religion as the origin of modern capitalism.[2] The beginnings of most of Parsons' later substantive themes - the family, child development, medical practice, economy, and modernity in general - can already be found in his discussion of Tönnies. Above all, this is where we find the juxtaposition of specific and unspecified attitudes and obligations as well as universal and non-universal institutional rules that later became two pairs of Parsons' pattern-variables.

Criteria of Social Normality

Both Durkheim and Parsons were more concerned with their visions of modern society. Durkheim's idea of organic solidarity and Parsons' idea of social integration had very similar intentions. In *The Division of Labor* and in *Suicide,* Durkheim's vision was ex-pressed as social coordination following rules of moral conduct.

This formulation was often abbreviated as collective conscience making individual acts subject to moral standards. In *The Elementary Forms,* Durkheim reformulated this principle as social practices following religious beliefs and values based on collective representations of the sacred. Formally, Parsons had a very similar vision of the interplay between individual motivation and social control in his theory of modernization seen as a transition from *Gemeinschaft-* to *Gesellschaft*-type social relations. This is where, according to Parsons, status-role bundles could be properly allocated which provided value-standards as the elusive solution to the problem of a normally functioning social system.

Parsons' thought moved from the individual to the collective level of sociological analysis. His theory of social action was formulated in Weberian terms of instrumental individual acts and internalized expressive value-orientations and external norms governing the selection of means. Parsons' interpretation of Durkheim in *The Structure of Social Action* was subjected to strong criticisms during the 1970's.[3] His nuanced response pointed out that his conceptual and interpretive positions had not been standing still.[4] Indeed, those positions were changing over the four decades since the publication of *The Structure.* Ever since the early formulation of his concept of voluntaristic social action, Parsons was trying to connect these abstractions of action frame of reference with the collective, institutional aspect of social systems and their normal functioning. Never completely satisfied with his obtained results, Parsons always held back readers and listeners from attempts at substantive interpretations of his conceptual schemes. Eventually, Parsons had to relinquish control of his creations to the new generation of students of the 1970's whose views were more inspired by C. Wright Mills. This new generation charged Parsons with a conservative bias towards the status quo.

To compensate, Parsons produced, somewhat belatedly, a grand evolutionist conception. Parsons believed that fundamental to any process of modernization, or "breaking out of [...] the primitive stage of societal evolution" were structural changes in social stratification, initially as a transition from status ascription to status achievement. Advanced societies of Europe and America are outcomes of three revolutions: the industrial, the democratic, and the educational revolution that were all marked by radical changes in the stratification systems of these societies.[5] The Industrial Revolution with its rapid changes in the occupational structure and rapid urbanization saw considerable strains and disruptions of smooth social functioning. Mass communication made debunking traditional ideas easier with no new ones offered by "the enormous development of popular education." Historic shifts in Western societies brought new "patterning of functional roles," but such patterning was not necessarily superior to the old one. More important for the overall functioning of the social system is the speed of change. Detrimental to the social system is the unevenness or incompleteness of the change process as it impinges on different social groups which results in conflicts among them.[6]

Durkheim's problem of criteria of morality and Parsons' of value-standards also pointed in the same direction. Durkheim spoke resolutely against Marxism in both its aspects of philosophy of history and as a practice of revolutionary social change. His concept of organic solidarity was rather based on the ethic of self-disciplined professional groups imbued with collective conscience. The notion of such social groups lends itself easily to an interpretation as groups of achieved occupational status groups not dissimilar from Weber's idea of status groups as groups of differential honor and prestige. The validity of this interpretation is indirectly supported by the argument that Durkheim's occupational groups do not constitute social classes.[7]

The originality of Durkheim's thought was in his endeavor to move the age-old questions of moral philosophy into the framework of empirical social science. First, in *The Division of Labor*, moral meant simply compliance with rules of law and custom whose ultimate authority was presumably the Ten Commandments. Moral rules were further specified as sacred religious values in *The Elementary Forms*. Durkheim's conception of sacred and profane served as a new version of his earlier distinction between normal and anomic or generally, pathological social practices as presented in *The Division of Labor, Suicide*, and *The Rules*. His criterion of social normality is revealed in his discussion of anomic forms of social solidarity. It was the idea of social coordination between the hierarchy of moderated satisfaction of human needs in consumption, on the one hand, and the hierarchy of complementary social functions performed by occupational groups (translated from French literally as "professional"), on the other.

Such coordination, according to Durkheim, was lacking, for example, in the anomic relationships between the living conditions of working men and those of their capitalist employers. Beyond that, Durkheim's turn to the study of primitive religion and his singular attention to it after his early denigration of all religious beliefs and practices can well be taken as a solution to the mystery of his "revelation of 1895." He must have realized that this pair of categories could serve as a general sociological model for the mechanism underlying all social change from mechanical to organic solidarity. Indeed, today's general use of the connection between beliefs and practices in explanations of human behavior and of social change can be seen retrospectively as supporting this thought.

Parsons expressed a similar idea of social reproduction in his concept of social integration judged by the criterion of adherence to the interpenetrating pairs of AGIL pattern-variables as functional imperatives for integrating the values of traditional community and modern society. Already in "Motivation of Economic Activity," Parsons highlighted, echoing Durkheim, moral sentiments that underlay conformity with institutional norms by which social action is evaluated. "This necessity of evaluation implies in turn the necessity of ranking, in the first place, qualities and achievements which are directly comparable [...] It is of crucial importance that the standards of ranking and their modes of application should, in the same social system, be relatively well integrated. [...] Every social system will have an institutionalized scale of stratification by which the different individuals in the system are ranked."[8]

Normative adherence to shared value-orientations was also implied in Parsons' principle of equilibrium in institutional societal exchange. Having extended Pareto's concept of social equilibrium from exchange relations of supply and demand to systemic social conditions in general, what Parsons meant by equilibrium was any systemic homeostasis. Whether as a balance between complementary role-expectations and performances or between economic supply and demand, these were all special cases of the general principle of homeostasis in living systems. This loss of sociological specificity in the original economic meaning of equilibrium tended to mask and outweigh Parsons' early concern with social injustice in capitalism. Instead, Parsons attempted to conceptualize power, influence, and commitment as quantifiable symbolic media of social values in social exchange by analogy with money.

Of these three concepts, commitment was perhaps the most interesting since it potentially connected Weber's idea of vocation as commitment to a moral-religious way of life with the problem of quantifiable standards of values in sociology. Apparently Parsons also tried to overcome the deep-seated conflict between his philosophic adherence to the Kantian idea of the cultural sphere being supra-social, and the political meaning that social action acquired in the 1970's when the abstraction of value-commitment was complemented with a more concrete notion of resource mobilization. If social action was the fundamental reality underlying all social relations, and if it was to be generally understood as politically rather than culturally motivated, then it must have been distribution of power in all its forms rather than symbolic media of exchange that was central to value-rationality as well as to social stratification.

In our reading of Durkheim, we considered *The Division of Labor* and *The Elementary Forms* as containing the most important seminal content of his work relevant to our purposes. For Parsons, we found such content mainly in his works up to the mid-

1950's that climaxed with *The Social System, Towards a General Theory of Action*, and the *Working Papers* where the AGIL four-function paradigm was constructed. Based on this reading, one obvious commonality between these two classics is their functionalist methodology.

Legitimate and Illegitimate Functional Explanations

Durkheim saw social institutions, including religion, as composed of elementary structural forms differentiated and reintegrated in the course of evolutionary social development. Thus by comparing modern Christianity with as simple a religion as possible, he hoped to arrive at the most elementary forms of religious life "that were permanent in all historic times and common to all humanity." Those basic elements, Durkheim believed, perform important social functions in all societies irrespective of their place on the ladder of social evolution.[9] This is the sense in which British cultural anthropologists later spoke of social functions and social functioning, meaning interdependence of primitive social institutions and their contributions to the survival and persistence of such societies over time.

According to Durkheim, social functions are independent of changing social structures being effects of their changes so that "a practice or a social institution changes its function without for this reason changing its nature."[10] Social structures can "hasten or retard development," but they cannot be changed without understanding their origins, their nature. Citing social division of labor as a prime example of both causal and functional explanation, Durkheim warned against teleological explanations of structures by functional needs. That would be a fallacious reversal of the logic of treating functions as effects. If it is necessary, an explanation of causes by collective representations must precede an explanation of effects. While effects derive their energy from causes, only occasionally an explanation by a cause also "requires its effect." Thus punishment follows crime as its consequence, but crime also has a "useful function" in that it maintains the high intensity of collective sentiments that determine punishment in the first place.[11] Occasionally Durkheim also spoke of social functions in the naturalistic physiological sense of specialized contributions made by morphological organs to the structural unity of social organism.

Durkheim modified Spencer's purely biological functionalism allowing for biological analogies and perspectives only to a point, as instruments of conceptualizing social facts, but not as models for social theories proper.[12] For him, functional imagery meant a method of explaining social outcomes, or effects, of changes in morphological social structures. While also recognizing the importance of providing causal explanations of origins of such structures, Durkheim devoted his main attention to correcting the widely spread practice of his time to confuse legitimate functional explanations with teleological ones, notably in Comte and Spencer. In fact, if we follow the logic of Durkheim's functionalism, any sociological study must consist mainly in combining observed changes of social structures with effects of those changes. Durkheim did point out that causal explanations of social structural changes would help sociologists correctly to classify them, and thus also facilitate their functional explanations. Nevertheless, it was his correction of the logic of functional explanations after Comte's and Spencer's teleology that remains Durkheim's original methodological contribution.

It must also be admitted that ambivalent and plainly contradictory statements can be found throughout Durkheim's *Rules*. If functional and causal explanations must be done separately, why should they also be combined? If teleological explanations from needs to structural effects were inadmissible, why demonstrate the utility of crime? *The Elementary Forms* did not differentiate clearly between social functions of religion and its causes.[13] In terms of *The Rules of Sociological Method*, this meant a coincidence of functional and causal explanations. Contemporary functions of primitive sacred beliefs and practices coincided with their origin as an antecedent (morphological) cause. While *The Division of La-*

bor was highly acclaimed by contemporaries, *The Elementary Forms of the Religious Life* was not received well by critics.

Anthropologists found that the conclusions of Durkheim's study were not warranted by its empirical evidence, itself presented in an arbitrary fashion. They noted that this work was speculative and deductive rather than a result of empirical study based on observation of facts as prescribed in *The Rules of Sociological Method*. The critics also rejected Durkheim's evolutionary assumptions adopted from Comte and Spencer as undermining his study of primitive religion. They called Durkheim a pseudo-historian for his equating of history with social evolution and for an "error fatal in consequences" in treating contemporaries of Central Australia as practicing a most primitive form of religion.[14]

Radcliffe-Brown was mistaken in characterizing this essentially biological conception of functionalism as the only one used by Durkheim.[15] Durkheim explicitly objected to this usage in *The Rules*. For him functionalism meant primarily explanations of effects of (morphological) social structures, notably of social solidarity as the effect of the division of labor. It was this naturalistic meaning of social functions and dysfunctions used by Malinowski and Radcliffe-Brown that Parsons adopted. It included both structural interdependence and process. It was meant to explain incremental stages of evolutionary development as combinations of institutional structural changes. Parsons was rather slow in recognizing that "structure and function were not correlative concepts on the same level"[16] Merton had hoped that "the concept of dysfunction, which implies the concept of strain, stress, and tension on the structural level [would provide] an analytical approach to the study of dynamics and change."[17] However, he fell into the same naturalistic functionalism when he found a number of "latent positive functions" in political machines.[18]

Parsons' understanding of the categories of system, subsystem, structure, and process was similar to the modern understanding of these terms in General System Theory. Today, the naturalistic realist view of systems as things is rejected in favor of its analytical conception as a tool for dealing with complexity.

According to this approach, reality is neither systemic nor non-systemic, and only our methods of treating real objects and such representations of them are either systemic or not.[19] This modeling aspect in Parsons was often lost in the more or less empiricist debate on functionalism in the 1960's and 1970's. Such interpretations went against the spirit if not the letter of Parsons' legacy. Parsons' seminal contribution to sociology was somewhere else. The enduring quality of his sociological legacy lies in some of its invaluable principles and innovative conceptual language.

If we overlook Parsons' attempts to reinterpret all elements of a social system in action terms, we can find their proper and specific place as elements of the general sociological process of modernization as transition from *Gemeinschaft* to *Gesellschaft*-type social relationships. Structurally this evolutionary mechanism is quite similar to that found in Durkheim's work. Indeed, where Durkheim spoke of beliefs, Parsons highlighted value orientations and role expectations that are but current beliefs projected into the future. And where Durkheim spoke of practices, Parsons had social action in its early voluntaristic rather than later ephemeral abstract sense. This was the same four-point general scheme of a structural social process that Coleman later modified as a model of rational choice.[20]

Sociology, Ethical and Logical

Durkheim's entire intellectual career was centered on the sociological investigation of morality. His works in the sociology of religion, above all *The Elementary Forms*, continued and supplemented his earlier *Division of Labor*. On the face of it, it marked his recognition of religion as the primordial cultural institution and a legitimate subject-matter of sociological study. It also marked a change in the empirical foundation of Durkheim's sociology of morality from the man-made, time-bound norms of statutory law to the timeless and sacred norms and values of religion. But there was more than that to Durkheim's "revelation of 1895" that produced eventually *The Elementary Forms*. Durkheim's empirical cultural anthropological work with primitive religion allowed him to add sacred beliefs and practices as crucial elements of evolutionary social development from mechanical to organic solidarity only implied in his earlier work. The morality of collective conscience – now renamed collective representations – and modern religious practices gave a practical, actionable meaning to the achievement of organic solidarity in the West as the outcome of division of labor. Durkheim therefore refrained from using the term social solidarity after *The Division of Labor*, and spoke instead of attachment to the group, love of society, general or collective effervescence, and collective ferment.

Despite attempts at its revival, Parsons' structural-functional sociology still stands largely for an abstract and sterile Grand Theory incapable of guiding social research, marred by his conservative political bias and by a plethora of inconsistencies blocking an understanding of his single works let alone their entire corpus. The second half of Parsons' intellectual career was based mostly on abstract AGIL categories that appeared to have a rather tangential connection with his early idea of voluntaristic social action. Parsons used the AGIL paradigm extensively in what looked like a structural surrogate of functional imperatives in both static and dynamic sociological perspectives. Critics concluded that these categories were merely formal place holders whose substantive meaning was mostly unclear. What, then, is the significance of Parsons' classical sociology?

The intellectual roots of Parsons' concern with general sociological categories go back to the years of his graduate work and instructorship at Harvard in the 1920's and early 1930's where he was influenced by Whitehead's system metaphysics. That influence was reinforced by the exemplary social-science applications of a system approach in Pareto and Schumpeter whose ideas were enthusiastically advanced by L. J. Henderson, the young Parsons' mentor at Harvard. The epistemology of grounding sociological theory of any level of generality - and thus the already abstract conception of the social system - in a still more abstract general theory of social action originated in Whitehead's philosophy of science, in particular, in the idea of a cate-gorial frame of reference. Combined with Pareto's notion of con-ceptual scheme, this idea was called to guide any theoretical in-terpretation of empirical facts, albeit at different levels, as well as their choice in the first place.[21]

Parsons never claimed his structural-functional program to be a method of empirical social research always warning against the fallacy of misplaced concreteness. All charges of the empirical sterility of Parsons' work, and the less empirically di-rected charges, like that of not being able to account for social conflict, may be missing the main point of his work. Parsons worked mostly on the conceptual level of developing general so-ciology, building a system of sociological categories that could guide sociologists in more specialized fields. In criticizing Weber's notion of ideal types, Parsons argued that it was atomistic and therefore falling short of the requirement necessary for a concep-tual scheme to be used as a frame of reference since the elements of such a frame must form an interrelated system.[22]

The work in this direction can, no doubt, be further im-proved by following Parsons' principle of systemic bilateral inter-penetration.[23] Parsons occasionally used the term "interlarding" in the same sense in the context of social stratification.[24] He ap-parently adopted the systemic idea of interpenetration from We-ber's categories of the relation between religious ethics and the world, and he invoked it as early as "The Place of Ultimate Val-ues in Sociological Theory." Münch attributes this idea to Kant,[25] but it may go even further back, to Aristotle.[26] Indeed, Marx pre-sented exchange and distribution as (mutually interpenetrated) middle terms of a standard syllogism where general-societal pro-duction and singular-individual consumption were pure polar terms.[27] Mediating bilateral interpenetration of polar opposites is a constructive systemic principle of greater complexity than either Kantian polar dichotomies or Hegelian triads of (unilateral) tran-scendental supersession (*Aufhebung*), and it can be seen as incor-porating them both.

After Parsons, there is no going back to Weber's presystemic ideal types or to pre-Weberian non-modeling conceptual language indistinguishable from substantive notions, let alone purely descriptive language games. Parsons' concept of combining social structures and processes in systemic development and his overall modeling approach to complex social relationships are now integral parts of the language of social sciences. Although his own conceptual schemes and their graphic representations leave much to be desired,[28] the principle itself of systemic conceptual models, or frames of reference, and the practice of using system models clearly earn Parsons a unique place in sociological thought.

Notes

[1] Parsons ((1937/1968, p. 694).
[2] Parsons (1937/1968, pp. 686-694).
[3] Pope, Cohen and Hazelring (1975).
[4] Parsons (1974).
[5] Parsons (1964, p. 342-344; 1971).
[6] Parsons (1942/1954c, pp. 127-131).
[7] See Grusky and Sørensen (1998), Grusky and Weeden (2001).
[8] Parsons (1940/1954a, pp. 53-55).
[9] Durkheim (1912/1965, pp. 13-21, 38, 462-463).
[10] Durkheim (1894/1982, p. 120).
[11] Durkheim (pp. 121-124, 131).
[12] Durkheim (1888/1978a, pp. 54-58).
[13] Durkheim (1912/1965, pp. 465-467, 473-474); cf. Pickering (1984, pp. 171-172).
[14] See van Gennep (1975), Goldenweiser (1975, p. 211), (Richard, 1975), Evans-Pritchard (1981, pp. 153-169).
[15] Radcliffe-Brown (1935/1952, pp. 178-187).
[16] Parsons (1970/1977a, p. 51; 1971/1977, p. 282).
[17] Merton ((1948/1967, p. 107).
[18] Merton (1949/1967, pp. 126-136). More on this in Smikun (2000).
[19] Dubrovsky (2004).
[20] Coleman (1986, 1990).
[21] Parsons (1970/1977b); cf. Fararo (1976), Camic (1987, 1989).
[22] Parsons (1937/1968, pp. 601-610, 634-640; 1947, pp. 8-29).
[23] Parsons (1935/1991, p. 257).
[24] Parsons (1953/1954, pp. 401, 410-411, passim)
[25] Münch (1981).
[26] See Dubrovsky (1999).

27 Marx (1857-1858/1973, p. 89).
28 Cf. Lynch (1991)

9

Institutional Obstacles to Fair Exchange

As described paradigmatically by Adam Smith, Market has been the main institution of mediated social exchange for much of human history. Although parties to market transactions are driven by self-interest, by virtue of free competition the sum-total of their actions is supposed to result in the best being rewarded and the worst punished. It is well known today that competition is never perfect, and that markets can run away resulting in a national economic disaster – as the Great Depression of 1929 and the financial crisis of 2008 showed. The belief in the miraculous invisible hand of Market as an institution of impersonal class exchange was shaken by Marx and finally shattered by Keynes. It is generally believed today that in addition to the free Market as an institution of exchange of class interests, it is the primary job of the Government to plan differential economic policies that would make structures of class interests conform better to structures of status groups.

Yet since the 1990's, when the Glass-Steagall Act was repealed, big banking and investment brokerage corporations have been allowed to engage freely in opaque off-the-books proprietary trading. They continue to transform what in principle was supposed to be a public utility into a private world-wide casino operation using OPM (other people's money) as it is known in the financial industry. Lacking government control, the small number of these banks and brokerage houses grew within two decades into "too big to fail" behemoths. The risky outcomes of their legalized large-scale gambling taking advantage of numerous less-than-sophisticated investors holds hostage the lives of millions of people in the United States and throughout the world. The US government whose job it is to subject all public interest to strict controls does not dare to touch these financial institutions.

Market, Planning, and Corporation

The two major historic institutions of social exchange of class interests – free Market and central Planning - underlying the capitalist and the socialist economic systems are based on opposite principles: purely competitive profit-seeking in free Market and purely cooperative equal exchange in central government Planning. These two principles can never be reconciled on their own. Both of them are still heavily laden with the ideological baggage of the 20th century. The institution of market and free Market is seen by the state as fundamentally anarchic and incapable of regulating exchange of public goods. In turn, central Planning is seen by Market – mainly financial, commodity, and real estate - as an unnecessary interference disrupting their free operation.

Both socialism and laissez-faire capitalism failed historically in their pure forms. Instead concepts of various mixed varieties of social systems have been proposed as describing what actually works in most of the world today. They go under different derivations of the old names – market socialism, state capitalism, planned market economy, capitalism with (socialist) Chinese characteristics, and the like. This is an awkward language, but there is a reason for its continued use. They all try to combine features of free market competition and comprehensive centralized planning

Central socialist state Planning was supposed to eliminate the anarchy, the uncertainties, and the wastefulness of capitalist business cycles endemic to purely market economic systems. By rationally allocating capital and human resources, comprehensive centralized state planning in the interest of all people was supposed to eradicate the imbalances among various branches of national economy inevitably created under capitalist Market conditions, especially in their monopolistic form that subvert the efficiency of the ideal market price mechanism. In so doing, central state planning would correct the perennial unevenness of capitalist economic development.

Yet, this is not how Planning turned out to work in the USSR, the country of victorious socialism. Comprehensive central Planning proved to be problematic in that huge country with its far-ranging natural conditions and diverse populations. No wonder the planned command economies of the USSR and the entire socialist camp imploded onto themselves. Only societies ideologically identifying with socialism such as China or Cuba continue to associate themselves with Planning as their main if not exclusive mechanism, and only economic systems ideologically identifying with capitalism such as that of the USA keep associating themselves exclusively with the market mechanism. Reality is quite different, however. There are two more forms serving as mediating institutions of exchange of class interests.

In contrast to smaller private companies, big Corporations do not hold immediate maximization of profits as their primary objective but rather long-term self-preservation and financial self-reliance by inviting investment. Every big Corporation requires its Board of Directors to be flexible and malleable in balancing planned use of known technologies, routine productivity strategies, stable markets, and efficiency with exploration of innovative technologies, experimental products, and new markets. For that reason, in addition to their shareholders, corporations are also controlled by the technostructure of professional managers, accountants and lawyers without whose expertise in long-term planning they would be exposed to substantial business risks.[1]

The presence of planning elements in big corporations led Galbraith to identify them with Planning as a sector of national economy standing in opposition to markets, and he was rightfully criticized on this point.[2] Still, Galbraith's concept of technostructure as big corporations' tool for dealing with uncertainties survived numerous critiques.[3] Owing to their investors' diverse interests the totality of Corporation is much better suited for balancing upper, middle, and lower class interests than the pure market mechanism typically operating for smaller and privately owned companies. On the other hand, due to the existence of substantial information asymmetries between corporate technostructure and other stakeholders, its accountability is often hampered by principal-agent problems such as potential conflicts of interest and moral hazard.

Technostructure abuses and other shortcomings of Corporation as an institution of exchange of class interests are - or can be – compensated by voluntary Participation typically in co-operatives and non-profit organizations that are essential parts of civil society. Participation historically represents the latest major institution of exchange of class interests. It emerged as a second, innovative form of bridging the gap between competitive Market and central government Planning complementing Corporation that until historically recent times has been playing this mediating role alone. Voluntary Participation is well on its way to becoming this missing counterbalancing force to the Corporation institution of class exchange.

The Idea of Countervailing Power

The idea of counterbalancing the enormous power of big corporations brings in mind Galbraith's concept of countervailing power. That concept was born more than half a century ago and referred empirically to institutions whose meaning may be quite different today. Consequently, the term countervailing power may allow for different interpretations, and one should be circumspect in using it. In his idea of the new industrial state, Galbraith made a clear distinction between traditional markets of classical and neoclassical economics driven by purely private self-interest, and big corporations dominated by technostructures. He implied that countervailing powers existed to both Market and Corporation. And if the Government (ideally) working for the public good was a countervailing power to markets driven by private self-interest, in the new industrial state there also had to be a countervailing power to big corporations.

Galbraith's concept of countervailing power did not primarily have to do with the achievement of material well-being but rather with high human ideals such as "social contentment," "minimization of social tension," "social harmonies," "social stability," and "the safeguards by which inherently weaker groups have found protection." Galbraith pointed out that this novel idea required a shift away from economists' conventional wisdom (also his term), and ended by saying bluntly that "men who resist any tampering with the rigidly idealized world of our ancestors" do not contribute to progressive social change.[4] According to him, the countervailing power to big corporations takes several different institutional forms of which labor unions representing the disadvantaged industrial workers and big retail chains representing consumers serve as prime examples. Galbraith presented labor unions as the major institutional framework of countervailing power to the original power of a few big technologically advanced manufacturing corporations. The role of the government was mainly in creating favorable conditions for such institutional frameworks to operate freely whether through antitrust legislation or by other means.[5]

It was mostly on these substantive-theoretical and public policy grounds rather than on conceptual or idealistic ones that critics found weaknesses in Galbraith's positions. One critic charged that Galbraith's claim of unions representing a strong countervailing power had "a limited plausibility but it rests on an enumeration of unions whose strength, and often existence, was due to the New Deal [...] Whatever the desirability of this type of organization, we cannot use government sponsored blocs as an illustration of the natural emergence of countervailing power".[6] A decade and a half after the concept of countervailing power was first introduced in *American Capitalism*, Galbraith himself noted the decline in the importance of labor unions as a countervailing power to big corporations. He described their various other useful and seemingly less useful functions in different industries[7] - without, however, getting to the core of this issues, namely, that rather than fair exchange of status groups' upper and lower class interests, organized labor represented only lower classes still following a basic socialist ideology of class struggle.

Milton Friedman did not fail to note the irony of this late stage in the 20th-century's labor movement in his overall critique of economic and political liberalism. He charged that rather than defending the interests of the working class as a whole, unions were defending only the interests of well-paid workers at the expense of lesser-paid ones, i.e., colluding with the corporate monopoly, or else even turning into an occasionally violent monopoly themselves.[8] As for consumer protection by retail chains that, according to Galbraith, stepped in where previously only manufacturers dominated, the situation had changed since the early 1950's.

By the time of the publication (in its first edition) of his *Free to Choose,* Friedman aimed his scathing critique at the ineffectiveness and wastefulness of government consumer protection agencies rather than at the big retail chains of the Sears (and now Walmart) kind that have become powerful business corporations in their own right.[9] In any event, this topic has more to do with fair distribution for status groups than with rational exchange of their class interests. Friedman also voiced his harsh criticism of the role of government in what Galbraith touted to be a facilitator to labor unions' countervailing power to big business. This was in fact the main content of Friedman's individualist economics.

When criticizing Galbraith and liberal economics in general, Friedman often appealed to Adam Smith and quoted from him copiously.[10] Yet Galbraith's novel ideas of countervailing power, of affluent society with its private-public imbalances, and of the new industrial state with its technostructures referred to big modern Corporations rather than to the world of entrepreneurial markets that Adam Smith had in mind. There is no denying that today more than ever big Corporations are controlled by commanding technostructures whose power often exceeds the power and reach of national governments.

Friedman's influential critique of liberalism has not directly challenged Galbraith's general idea of countervailing power itself. What was subjected to critique was the empirical meaning of this concept as relevant to the early 1950's, but the basic idea of countervailing power has not been invalidated. All the critiques – by Friedman and by others cited by him - were of the empirical rather than of the conceptual kind. If the idea of countervailing power is taken as a conceptual ideal type in Weber's sense rather than in the sense of empirical realism, then its ideological socialist connotations may fall by the side.

For the same reason, one must distinguish the highly beneficial historical role of Corporation in publicly traded corporations - where in principle anyone can be a shareholder - from the ways this idea can be distorted in real life, mainly due to the lack of effective competition from the still young sector of voluntary Participation. And if labor unions and retail chains of today cannot be the institutional frameworks for countervailing power to big corporations, perhaps some other institutions can. This is where Participation in cooperatives and non-profit organizations come in. Similar to central government Planning that has always been a balancing factor to the free operation of spontaneously forming Markets, Participation in cooperatives and nonprofits has all the makings of being the mirror image of big Corporations, as their obverse.

The Potential of Voluntary Participation

Weber's notion of ideal types may be a hundred years old, but it still remains a somewhat esoteric doctrine, especially for empirically-minded students of sociology. For this reason, applying Galbraith's notion of countervailing power to voluntary Participation may still run the risk of being interpreted as implying the socialist and communist critique of capitalism and of the labor movement as a form of class struggle. In point of fact, the opposite is true. The continuing growth of voluntarism and active Participation in cooperatives and nonprofits slowly but surely becomes an alternative to old-style labor movements. In any event, to avoid such connotations, we prefer to speak about the counterbalancing role of voluntary Participation in cooperatives and nonprofits as complementing and competing with big Corporations rather than as subverting them.

Even though they are deficient, the Market and the Planning institutions of class exchange also have their strengths, and they are indispensable in their own places. Their strength comes from their comprehensiveness and simplicity. While recognizing and praising the democratic nature of Corporation and Participation institutions of class exchange, we should not overlook the necessity of Market and Planning as its simple individualistic and collectivistic institutions. The Corporation and the Participation institutions of class exchange cannot stand on their own without Market and Planning providing their primary pure elements of competition and cooperation. Still, the effectiveness of both competitive Market and government Planning has increasingly been brought into question if for no other reason than growing transaction costs and intractable ideological conflicts among political elites. It is also unrealistic to expect social justice from what is now an obsolescent Welfare State fostering an immature and demoralizing mentality of paternalistic dependency.

Social justice in modern representative democracies is a matter of finding ways to reconcile and integrate conflicting class interests of unequal status groups that are supposed to be represented by political parties. Protest movements for social justice can do better than occupying streets, staging boycotts, or breaking windows. They can channel their energies into constructive goals of mutual help by voluntary Participation in productive non-profit organizations. That would complement the entrepreneurial energies of Corporation in business corporations and create an effective counterbalancing competition to their profit motive and their proclivity for monopolistic practices. There is no reason why mature non-profit enterprises mobilizing progressives, idealists, the unemployed, and the poor should not be able to compete successfully with big corporations in quality and price. Compelled by "the push of necessity and the pull of opportunity," the voluntary simplicity of service in non-profit organizations could be the best way to eradicate both unemployment and inflation, the inexorable double scourge of our failing social order modeled on outdated economic theories.

As a relatively new institution balancing investment in for-profit business Corporations, voluntary Participation in cooperatives and nonprofits should be able to turn out affordable products and services – not only in professional areas such as health care, college education and television programming, but also in manufacturing that may have been offshored, or that business corporations are not interested in, or overlook for some other reason. They should be able to produce decent housing, reliable transportation, nutritious food, environmentally friendly sources of energy, and other public goods available to all. Given freedom from taxation, this fourth sector of voluntary Participation could in principle do it more cheaply if not more efficiently. This balanced model has also been emerging on the international scale since the end of Cold War in various forms. It can be seen in core rich countries' foreign aid to periphery poor countries that promotes employment or in the European idea of two-speed economy where slower-speed countries have to inaugurate austerity programs as a condition for their financial bail-out. South-East Asia is a success story of periphery countries quickly developing from rags to riches owing primarily to the voluntary simplicity of their cheap and disciplined labor. They will surely leave behind the West if it continues to hold on to the aging unbalanced model of affluent corporate capitalism living side-by-side with mass unemployment, dependency, and poverty.

As a major part of civil society, voluntary Participation could create an effective competition to Corporation in the otherwise unemployment-prone big corporations. The idea of civil society is sometimes presented as opposed to economic and political institutions.[11] Apparently, such conceptualizations confuse settlement, industry, financial, and political class interests with Corporation and Planning institutions of their social exchange. Family and educational status groups also share these class interests. It would likewise be erroneous to associate the specificity of civil society consisting of non-profit and non-government organizations only with family or educational institutions.

Presenting the Participation institution of exchange as counterbalancing and complementing investment in big Corporations is justified by its enormous potential more than by what its somewhat disorganized structures of today's cooperatives and nonprofits may suggest. Non-profit organizations are often described as a third sector of a national economy in contradistinction from its private and public sectors. It is assumed that investment in big publicly traded Corporations belongs to the same private sector as Markets do, and that the Government's public sector stands in an opposition to them both. This assumption ignores the substantial difference between private and public class interests exchanged in these sectors.

Four Sectors of Exchange and Distribution

Both Market and Corporation are mechanisms for a free exchange of private class interests. However, financial, commodity, and real estate markets are basically private mechanisms for this social exchange. Investment in publicly traded Corporations, or joint-stock companies, was historically designed as a public mechanism for the exchange of such private class interests. The fact that private financiers are also allowed to incorporate their lending services, to raise their own capital, and to engage in proprietary trading blurs this fundamental distinction, and this may well be the single most decisive cause of the 2008 financial crisis. Having parasitically colonized this public mechanism of private class exchange, fundamentally unproductive yet powerful financial institutions continue to enjoy uncontrolled growth and a privileged status of being "too big to fail." They continue to hold entire national and international economies hostage and make them pay ransom with impunity in the form of bailouts. Having also "securitized" what was supposed to be targeted investments in productive business corporations, these financial power houses corrupted them too, making them part of their world-wide gambling enterprise.

Market and central government Planning are polar opposites being purely private and purely public institutions of class exchange. As an institution of exchange of class interests, Market lacks elements of Planning that are always present in corporate technostructures. In turn, government Planning lacks the elements of competition and private entrepreneurial interest that are always present in voluntary Participation in cooperatives and nonprofits even as they pursue public interest. Corporation and Participation institutions of exchange combine in themselves characteristics of both Market and central Planning. By investing in shares of joint-stock companies, people participate in a public concern. Yet, corporations provide returns on their investments in a purely private manner. For that reason corporate investment can be seen as a public sphere for exchange of status groups' private class interests, such as industry, settlement, political, and property-related ones.

By contrast, cooperatives and nonprofits are typically set up by private foundations or charities. It is for this reason empirical research of Cooperatives and nonprofits and NGOs is not an easy task. It has been observed that literature on them is "balkanized",[12] and that it "is based more on faith than fact:

There are relatively few detailed studies of what is happening in particular places or within specific organizations, few analyses of the impact of NGO practices on relations of power among individuals, communities, and the state, and little attention to the discourse within which NGOs are presented as the solution to problems of welfare service delivery, development, and democratization."[13] Yet their mission always has to do with public interest, be it environmental protection or decent living conditions for the disadvantaged.

Similar to state Planning, Participation is engaged in producing so-called collective or public goods. While their trustee boards are typically dominated by members of the upper classes apparently conscious of the need to maintain class structures that are more consistent with relevant status groups, formal technostructures have also been moving into positions of non-profit governance.[14] It is in this sense that voluntary Participation can be seen as a private sphere for exchange of status groups' public class interests. If that is so, Market and Planning must be considered as the first and the second sectors, while Corporation and Participation as the third and the fourth sectors, respectively.

Notes

[1] Galbraith (1967).
[2] See, for example, Tobin (1974).
[3] Keaney (2001), Dunn (2010).
[4] Galbraith (1954, pp. 2-6).
[5] Galbraith (2010, p. 121).
[6] Stigler (1954, p. 11).
[7] Galbraith (1967, pp. 271-290).
[8] Friedman (1962, pp. 123-124). Friedman and Friedman (1990, pp. 229-242).
[9] Friedman (1990, pp. 189-227).
[10] Friedman (1977, p.14), Friedman and Friedman (1990).
[11] See Skocpol (1996) for one analysis of such conceptualizations.
[12] Dimaggio and Anheier (1990, pp. 154).
[13] Fisher (1997).
[14] Cf. Dimaggio and Anheier (1990, pp. 141-142).

Bibliography

Abel, Thomas and William C. Cockerham (1993). Lifestyle or Lebensführung? Critical Remarks on the Mistranslation of Weber's 'Class, Status, Party'. *The Sociological Quarterly*, 34(3), 551-556.

Agresti, Alan (1984). *Analysis of Ordinal Categorical Data*. New York: Wiley.

Alford, C. Fred. (1985). Is Jürgen Habermas' Reconstructive Science Really Science? *Theory and Society*, 14 (3), pp. 321-340.

Althusser, Louis. (1965). *For Marx*. New York: Pantheon.

Árnason, Jóhann P. (1982). Universal Pragmatics and Historical Materialism. *Acta Sociologica*, 25(3), pp. 219-233.

Austin, John L. (1962). *How to Do Things with Words*. Oxford: Clarendon.

Baron-Cohen, Simon. (2011) *The Science of Evil: On empathy and the origins of human cruelty*. Basic Books.

_____ (2012). http://www.youtube.com/watch?v=nXcU8x_xK18

Baudrillard, Jean (1981). *For a Critique of the Political Economy of the Sign*. St.. Louis: Telos Press.

Bendix, Reinhard. (1962). *Max Weber: An Intellectual Portrait*. New York: Anchor Books, Doubleday.

Berger, Peter L., and Thomas Luckmann. (1967). *The Social Construction of Reality: A Treatise in the Sociology of Knowledge*. Garden City, NY: Doubleday.

Berle, Adolf and Gardiner Means. (1932/1967). *The Modern Corporation and Private Property*. New York: Harcourt, Brace and World.

Berry, Ruth E. and Williams, Flora L. (1987) Assessing the Relationship between Quality of Life and Marital and Income Satisfaction: A Path Analytic Approach, *Journal of Marriage and the Family* 49 (February): 107-116;.

Bian, Yanjie. (2002). Chinese Social Stratification and Social Mobility. *Annual Review of Sociology*, 28, 91-116.

Blalock Jr., H.M., (Ed.) (1971). *Causal Models in the Social Sciences*. Chicago: Aldine.

Blau, Peter M. (1960). Structural Effects. *American Sociological Review* 25, pp. 178-193.

_____ (1964). *Exchange and Power in Social Life*. New Brunswick, NJ: Transaction Books.

_____ (1977). *Inequality and Heterogeneity: A Primitive Theory of Social Structure*. New York: Free Press.

Blau, Peter M., and Otis Dudley Duncan. (1967). *The American Occupational Structure*. New York: Wiley.

Blau, Peter M., T. C. Blum, and J. E. Schwartz. (1982). Heterogeneity and intermarriage. *American Sociological Review* v.47 pp. 45–62

Blau, Peter M. and Joseph Schwartz (1984). *Crosscutting Social Circles: Testing a Macrostructural Theory of Intergroup Relations*. New Brunswick, NJ: Transaction

Publishers.

Blum, Fred H. (1944). Max Weber's Postulate of "Freedom" from Value Judgments. *American Journal of Sociology*, 50(1), 46-52.

Boswell, Terry, Cliff Brown, John Brueggemann, and T. Ralph Peters Jr. (2006). *Racial Competition and Class Solidarity*. Albany: State University of New York Press.

Bottomore, Tom. (1975). *Marxist Sociology*. New York: Holmes and Meier.

Bourdieu, Pierre. (1990). *The Logic of Practice*. Stanford, CA: Stanford University Press

Bulmer, Martin (2001). Social Measurement: What Stands in the Way? *Social Research*, 68(2), pp. 455-480.

Burawoy, Michael. (2005). The Return of the Repressed: Recovering the Public Face of U.S. Sociology, One Hundred Years On. *Annals of the American Academy of Political and Social Science*, Vol. 600 (Jul), pp. 68-85.

Camic, Charles. (1987). The Making of a Method: A Historical Reinterpretation of the Early Parsons. *American Sociological Review*, 52(4), 421-439.

_____ (1989). Structure after 50 years: The Anatomy of a Charter. *American Journal of Sociology*, 95(1), pp. 38-107.

Chan, Tak Wing and John H. Goldthorpe. (2004). Is There a Status Order in Contemporary British Society? *European Sociological Review*, 20, pp. 383-401.

_____ (2007). Social Status and Newspaper Readership. *American Journal of Sociology*, 112(4), pp. 1095-1134.

Carsten Oliver (1988). Ethnic Particularism and Class Solidarity: The Experience of Two Connecticut Cities. *Theory and Society*, 17(3), pp. 431-450.

Chikszentmihalyi, Mihaly and Eugene Rochberg-Halton (1981). *The Meaning of Things: Domestic Symbols and the Self*. New York: Cambridge University Press.

Cicourel, Aaron V. (1973). *Cognitive Sociology: Language and Meaning in Social Interaction*. London: Penguin.

Cohen, Gerald A. (1979). The Labor Theory of Value and the Concept of Exploitation. *Philosophy and Public Affairs*. Vol. 8(4), pp. 338-360.

_____ (1983). More on Exploitation and the Labour Theory of Value. *Inquiry*. *Vol.* 26, pp. 309-331.

Cohen, Jean L. (1985). Strategy or Identity: New Theoretical Paradigms and Contemporary Social Movements. *Social Research* 52(4), pp. 663-716.

Cohen, Jere. (1975). Reply to Parsons. *American Sociological Review*, 40, pp. 670-674.

Cohen, Ira J. (2000). Theories of Action and Praxis. In B. S. Turner (Ed.), *The Blackwell Companion to Social Theory* (pp. 73-111). (2nd ed.). Malden, MA: Blackwell.

Coleman, James S. (1986). Social Theory, Social Research, and a Theory of Action, *American Journal of Sociology* v.91, pp. 1309-1335.

_____ (1990). *Foundations of Social Theory*. Cambridge, MA: Harvard University Press.

Colletti, Lucio. (1975). *Introduction*. In *Karl Marx. Early Writings* (pp. 7-57). New York: Vintage.

Dallmayr, Fred. (1988). Habermas and Rationality. *Political Theory*, Vol. 16, No. 4, pp. 553-579.

Davis, James A. and Thomas W. Smith (1992). *The NORC General Social Survey*. Newbury Park: Sage.

Dimaggio, Paul J., and Helmut K. Anheier. (1990). The Sociology of Nonprofit Organizations and Sectors. *Annual Review of Sociology* Vol. 16, pp. 137-159.

Donati, Paolo. (1981). Organization between movement and institution. *Social Science Information* 23 (4/5), pp. 837-859.

Douthat, Ross (2013). "Late Marriage and Its Consequences." *New York Times*, March 22, 2013.

Dubrovsky, Vitaly. (1999). Beyond Duality: From Opposition to Constructive Attribution. *Proceedings of the Forty-Second Meeting of the International Society for Systems Sciences*. Louisville, KY.

_____ (2004). Toward system principles: general system theory and the Alternative approach. *System Research and Behavioral Science,* 21(2), pp. 109-122.

Duncan, Otis D. (1961). A Socioeconomic Index for all Occupations. In J. Reiss, Jr. (Ed.), *Occupations and Social Status* (pp. 109–138). New York: Free Press of Glencoe.

Dunn, Stephen P. (2010). *The Economics of John Kenneth Galbraith: Introduction, Persuasion, and Rehabilitation*. Cambridge University Press.

Durkheim, Emile. (1885). Gumplowitz, Ludwig. Grundriss der Soziologie. *Revue philosophique de la France et l'étranger,* XX, 625-634.

_____ (1885/1978). [Review of Albert Schaeffle, Bau und Leben des Sozialen Körpers: Erster Band]. In M. Traugott (Ed.). *Emile Durkheim on Institutional Analysis*, (pp. 93-114). Chicago: University of Chicago Press.

_____ (1886). Les Etudes de science sociale. *Revue philosophique de la France et l'étranger,* XXII, 61-80.

_____ (1887/1986-1987). The Positive Science of Ethics in Germany. *History of Sociology,* 6-7, 191-251.

_____ (1888). Suicide et natalité: étude de statistique morale. *Revue philosophique de la France et l'étranger,* XXVI, 446-463.

_____ (1888/1978b). Introduction to the Sociology of the Family. In M. Traugott (Ed.). *Emile Durkheim on Institutional Analysis*, (pp. 205-228). Chicago: University of Chicago Press.

_____ (1889/1978). [Review of Ferdinand Tönnies, Gemeinschaft und Gesellschaft]. In M. Traugott (Ed.). *Emile Durkheim on Institutional Analysis*, (pp. 115-122). Chicago: University of Chicago Press.

_____ (1893/1983). The Origins of Law. In S. Lukes and A. Sculli (Eds.). *Durkheim and the Law* (pp. 146-157). New York: St. Martin's Press.

_____ (1893/1984). *The Division of Labor in Society*. New York: Free Press.

_____ (1894/1982). The Rules of Sociological Method. In S. Lukes (Ed.). *The Rules of Sociological Method and Selected Textes on Sociology and Its Method* (pp. 31-163). New York: Free Press.

_____ (1897/1951). *Suicide*. New York: Free Press.

_____ (1898/1960). Prefaces to L'Année Sociologique. In K. Wolff (Ed.). *Emile Durkheim. A Collection of Essays with Translations and a Bibliography* (pp. 341-353). Columbus, OH: Ohio State University Press.

_____ (1898-1900/1983). *Professional Ethics and Civic Morals*. Westport, CN: Greenwood Press.

_____ (1899/1975). Concerning the Definition of Religious Phenomena. In W.S.F. Pickering (Ed.). *Durkheim on Religion. A Selection of Readings with Bibliographies and Introductory Remarks* (pp. 74-99). London: Routlage & Kegan Paul.

_____ (1900/1981). The Realm of Sociology as a Science. *Social Forces,* 59, pp. 1054-1070.

_____ (1901/1983). The Evolution of Punishment. In S. Lukes and A. Sculli (Eds.). *Durkheim and the Law* (pp. 102-132). New York: St. Martin's Press.
_____ (1902-1903/1961). *Moral Education.* New York: Free Press.
_____ (1903/1982). Sociology and the Social Sciences. In S. Lukes (Ed.) *The Rules of Sociological Method and Selected Texts on Sociology and Its Method* (pp. 175-208). New York: Free Press
_____ (1905/1982). The Role of General Sociology. In S. Lukes (Ed.). *The Rules of Sociological Method and Selected Texts on Sociology and Its Method* (pp. 255-256). New York: Free Press.
_____ (1908a/1982). Debate on Political Economy and Sociology. In S. Lukes (Ed.). *The Rules of Sociological Method and Selected Texts on Sociology and Its Method* (pp. 229-235) New York: Free Press.
_____ (1909/1978). Sociology and the Social Sciences. In M. Traugott (Ed.). *Emile Durkheim on Institutional Analysis* (pp. 71-87). Chicago: University of Chicago Press.
_____ (1912/1965). *The Elementary Forms of the Religious Life.* New York: Free Press.
_____ (1914/1960). The Dualism of Human Nature and Its Social Conditions. In K. Wolff (Ed.). *Emile Durkheim. A Collection of Essays with Translations and a Bibliography* (pp. 325-340). Columbus, OH: Ohio State University Press.
_____ (1924/1953). *Sociology and Philosophy.* Glencoe: Free Press.
_____ (1955/1983). *Pragmatism and Sociology.* Cambridge: Cambridge University Press.
Durkheim, Emile and Marcel Mauss. (1963). *Primitive Classifications.* Chicago: University of Chicago Press.
Dworkin, Ronald. (1986). *Law's Empire.* Harvard University Press.
Echeverria, Rafael. (1978). Critique of Marx's 1857 Introduction. *Economy and Society,* 7(4), pp. 333-366.
_____ (1980). The Concrete and the Abstract In Marx's Method. A Reply to Carver. *Economy and Society,* 9(2), pp. 204-217.
Ehring, Douglas. (1987). Cohen, Exploitation, and Theft. *Dialogue.* Vol. 26(2), pp. 299-308.
Eisen, Arnold. (1978). The meanings and confusions of Weberian 'rationality'. *British Journal of Sociology,* 29(1), pp. 57-70.
Elgin, Duane. (1993). *Voluntary Simplicity: Toward a Way of Life That is Outwardly Simple, Inwardly Rich.* New York: Quill.
_____ (2009). *The Living Universe.* San Francisco: Berrett-Koehler Publishers.
Engels, Frederick. (1972). *The Origin of the Family, Private Property, and the State.* New York: International Publishers.
_____ (1975). Outlines of a Critique of Political Economy. In *Karl Marx and Frederick Engels. Collected Works.* Volume 3 (pp. 418-443). New York: International Publishers.
Espeland, Wendy Nelson and Mitchell L. Stevens (1998). Commensuration as a Social Process. *Annual Review of Sociology* v.24, pp. 313-343.
Evans-Pritchard, Edward Evan. (1981). *A History of Anthropological Thought.* New York: Basic Books.
Fararo, Thomas J. (1976). On the Foundations of the Theory of Action in Whitehead and Parsons. In J. Loubser et al. (Eds.). *Explorations in General Theory in Social Science,* Vol. 2 (pp. 90-122). New York: The Free Press.

Feuerbach, Ludwig. (1972). *The Fiery Brook: Selected Writings of Ludwig Feuerbach*. Garden City: Anchor Books.

_____ (1975). *Essence of Christianity: Milestones of Thought*. Frederick Ungar.

Filloux, Jean-Claude. (1977). *Durkheim et le socialisme*. Geneve: Librarie Droz.

Fisher, William F. (1997). Doing Good? The Politics and Antipolitics of NGO Practices. *Annual Review of Anthropology*, Vol. 26, pp. 439-464.

Frenzen, Jonathan, Paul M. Hirsch and Philip C. Zerillo. (1994). Consumption, Preferences and Changing Lifestyles. Pp. 401-425 in Smelser, Neil J. and Richard Swedberg (Editors). *Handbook of Economic Sociology*. Russel Sage Foundation.

Friedman, John. (1987). *Planning in the Public Domain: From Knowledge to Action*. Princeton University Press.

Friedman, Milton. (1962). *Capitalism and Freedom*. Chicago: University of Chicago Press.

_____ (1977). *From Galbraith to Economic Freedom*. London: Institute of Economic Affairs.

Friedman, Milton and Rose Friedman. (1990). *Free to Choose: A Personal Statement*. New York: Harcourt, Inc.

Friedman, Thomas L. (2005). *The World is Flat: A Brief History of the Twenty-first Century*. New York: Farrar, Straus and Giroux.

Galbraith, John Kenneth. (1952). *American Capitalism: The Concept of Countervailing Power*. Hamish Hamilton.

_____ (1954). Countervailing Power. *American Economic Review*, Vol. 44. No. 2 (May), pp. 1-6.

_____ (2010). *The Affluent Society and Other Writings 1952-1967*. New York: The Library of America.

_____ (1967). *The New Industrial State*. New York: Signet.

Garfinkel, Harvey, and Harvey Sacks. (1970). On Formal Structures of Practical Actions. In J.C. McKinney and E.A. Tiryakian (Eds.). *Theoretical Sociology*, pp. 338-366. New York: Appleton Century Crofts.

Giddens, Anthony. (1984). *The Constitution of Society: Outline of the Theory of Structuration*. Berkeley: University of California Press.

Goffman, Erving. (1959). *The Presentation of Self in Everyday Life*. New York: Doubleday Books.

_____ (1967). *Interaction Ritual: Essays on Face-to-face Behavior*. New York: Pantheon Books.

_____ (1971). *Relations in Public: Microstudies of the Public Order*. New York: Harper & Row.

Goldenweiser, A. A. (1975). [Review. 'Les Formes élémentaires de la vie religieuse']. In W.S.F. Pickering (Ed.). *Durkheim on Religion. A Selection of Readings with Bibliographies and Introductory Remarks* (pp. 209-227). London: Routlage & Kegan Paul.

Goldthorpe, John H. (1996). The Quantitative Analysis of Large-Scale Data-Sets and Rational Choice Theory: For a Sociological Alliance. *European Sociological Review*, 12(2), pp. 98-126.

_____. (1998). Rational Action Theory for Sociology. *British Journal of Sociology*, 49(2), pp. 167-192.

_____. (2002). Occupational Sociology, Yes; Class Analysis, No. Comment on Grusky and Weeden's Research Agenda. *Acta Sociologica* 45, pp. 211-223.

_____. (2007). *On Sociology. Second Edition. Volume One. Critique and Program.* Stanford University Press.

Gross, Neil. (2009). A Pragmatist Theory of Social Mechanisms. *American Sociological Review* 74(3), pp. 358-379.

Grusky, David B. and Jesper B. Sørensen, (1998). Can class analysis be salvaged? *American Journal of Sociology* v.103 (5), pp. 1187 – 234.

Grusky, David B., and Kim A. Weeden. (2001). Decomposition without Death: A Research Agenda for a New Class Analysis. *Acta Sociologica v.* 44, pp. 203-218.

Gusfield, Joseph R. (1984). Social Movements and Social Change: Perspectives of Linearity and Fluidity. *Research in Social Movements, Conflict and Change* 4, pp. 317-339.

Habermas, Jürgen. (1976). Some Distinctions in Universal Pragmatics: A Working Paper. *Theory and Society*, 3(2): pp. 155-167.

_____ 1979. *Communication and Evolution of Society.* Boston: Beacon Press.

_____ (1984). The Theory of Communicative Action. Volume One. Reason and Rationalization of Society. Boston: Beacon Press.

_____ (1987). The Theory of Communicative Action. Volume Two. Lifeworld and System: A Critique of Functionalist Reason. Boston: Beacon Press.

Hatt, Paul K. and Virginia Ktsanes. (1952). Patterns of American Stratification as Reflected In Selected Social Science Literature. *American Sociological Review*, 17, pp. 670-679.

Hayek. F.A. (1944/1976). The Road to Serfdom. London, Rutledge & Kegan.

_____ (1960) *The Constitution of Liberty.* Chicago: University of Chicago Press.

Hechter, Michael and Satoshi Kanazawa. (1997). Sociological Rational Choice Theory. *Annual Review of Sociology,* 23, pp. 191-214.

Hegel, G. W. F. (1958). *Hegel's Philosophy of Right,* (T.M. Knox, Trans., Notes). London: Oxford University Press.

_____ (1975). *Hegel's Logic, Being Part of the Encyclopedia of the Philosophical Sciences* (1830). (W. Wallace, Trans,), Oxford: Clarendon.

Homans, George Caspar. (1961). *Social Behavior: Its Elementary Forms.* New York: Harcourt Brace Jovanovich.

_____ (1967). *The Nature of Social Science.* New York: Harcourt, Brace & World.

Inkeles, Alex. (1968). Social Change in Soviet Russia, Cambridge, Harvard University Press.

Jacoby, William G. (1991). *Data Theory and Dimensional Analysis.* London: Sage.

Jaspers, Karl. (1964). *Three Essays: Leonardo, Descartes, Max Weber.* New York: Harcourt, Brace and World.

Jones, Robert Alun. (1974). Durkheim's Response to Spencer: An Essay Toward Historicism in the Historiography of Sociology. *The Sociological Quarterly*, 15, 341-358.

_____ (1977). On Understanding a Sociological Classic. *American Journal of Sociology,* 83, 279-319.

_____ (1994). The Positive Science of Ethics in France: German Influences on 'De la division du travail social' *Sociological Forum*, 9(1), pp. 37-57.

Kalberg, Stephen. (2002). Introduction to The Protestant Ethic. In *Max Weber. The Protestant Ethic and the Spirit of Capitalism* (pp. xi-lxxvi). Los Angeles: Roxbury.

Keaney, Michael. (2001). *Economist with a Public Purpose: Essays in Honor of John Kenneth Galbraith.* Routledge.

Kelly, Colm. (1990). Methods of Reading and the Discipline of Sociology. *Canadian Journal of Sociology*, 15, pp. 301-324.

Lee, Eun Sul, Ronald N. Forthoffer, and Ronald J. Lorimor. (1992). Analyzing Complex Survey Data. Sage University paper series on Quantitative Applications in the Social Sciences, 07-071 Beverly Hills: Sage.

Lenski, Gerhard E. (1966). *Power and Privilege. A Theory of Social Stratification.* New York: McGraw-Hill.

Letwin, William (Ed.) (1983). *Against equality: readings on economic and social policy.* London: Macmillan.

Liao, Tim Futing (1994). *Interpreting Probability Models: Logit, Probit, and Other Generalized Linear Models.* Thousand Oaks: Sage.

Lieberson, Stanley (1985). *Making It Count: The Improvement of Social Research and Theory.* Berkeley: University of California Press.

_____ (2002). Barking Up the Wrong Branch: Scientific Alternatives to the Current Model of Sociological Science (with Freda B. Lynn). *Annual Review of Sociology* 28, pp. 1-19.

Lukács, Georg. (1920/1967). *History and Class Consciousness.* London: Merlin Press.

Lukes, Steven. (1985). *Emile Durkheim. His Life and Work.* Stanford University Press.

Lynch, Michael. (1991). Pictures or Nothing? Visual Constructs in Social Theory. *Sociological Theory,* 9(1), pp. 1-21.

Lyotard, Jean-François. (1984). *The Postmodern Condition: A Report on Knowledge.* Minneapolis: University of Minnesota Press.

Mack, Raymond W., Linton Freeman and Seymour Yellin. (1957). *Social Mobility: Thirty Years of Research and Theory; an Annotated Bibliography.* Syracuse: Syracuse University Press.

Macy, Michael W. (1988). Value Theory and the 'Golden Eggs': Appropriating the Magic of Accumulation. *Sociological Theory.* Vol. 6, pp. 131-152.

Mah, Harold E. (1986). Karl Marx in Love: The Enlightenment, Romanticism, and Hegelian Theory in the Young Marx. *History of European Ideas,* 7(5), pp. 489-507.

Mannheim, Karl. (1985). *Ideology and Utopia.* New York: Harcourt Brace Jovanovich.

Marshall, T. H. (1950). *Citizenship and Social Class.* Cambridge: Cambridge University Press.

_____ (1977). *Class, Citizenship and Social Development.* London: Heinemann.

Marx, Karl. (1843/1975a). Critique of Hegel's Doctrine of the State. In *Karl Marx. Early Writings* (pp. 57-198). New York: Vintage.

_____ (1843/1975b). Letters from the Franco-German Yearbook. In *Karl Marx. Early Writings* (pp. 199-209). New York: Vintage.

_____ (1843/1975c). On the Jewish Question In *Karl Marx. Early Writings* (pp. 211-241). New York: Vintage.

_____ (1843-1844/1975). A Contribution to the Critique of Hegel's Philosophy of Right. Introduction. In *Karl Marx. Early Writings* (pp. 243-257). New York: Vintage.

_____ (1844/1975a). Excerpts from James Mill's Elements of Political Economy. In Karl Marx. *Early Writings* (pp. 259-278). New York: Vintage.

_____ (1844/1975b). Economic and Philosophical Manuscripts. In *Karl Marx. Early Writings* (pp. 279-400). New York: Vintage.

_____ (1844/1975c). Critical Notes on the Article "The King of Prussia and Social

Reform. By a Prussian. In *Karl Marx. Early Writings* (pp. 401-420). New York: Vintage.

_____ (1845/1975). Concerning Feuerbach. In *Karl Marx. Early Writings* (pp. 421-423). New York: Vintage.

_____ (1846/1968). Marx to P.V. Annenkov, December 28, 1846. In K. Marx and F. Engels. *Selected Works in One Volume* (pp. 669-679). New York: International Publishers.

_____ (1849/1968). Wage Labor and Capital. In K. Marx and F. Engels. *Selected Works in One Volume* (pp. 72-94). New York: International Publishers.

_____ (1852/1974). The Eighteenth Brumaire of Louis Bonaparte. In Karl Marx. *Surveys from Exile. Political Writings* Volume II (pp. 143-249). New York: Vintage.

_____ (1857-1858/1973). *Grundrisse. Foundations of the Critique of Political Economy.* New York: Vintage.

_____ (1859/1975). Preface (to A Contribution to the Critique of Political Economy). In Karl Marx. *Early Writings* (pp. 424-428). New York: Vintage.

_____ (1861-1863/1971). *Theories of Surplus-Value.* (Vols. 1-3). Moscow: Progress.

_____ (1867/1977). *Capital. A Critique of Political Economy.* Volume One. New York: Vintage.

_____ (1885/1981). *Capital. A Critique of Political Economy.* Volume Two. New York: Vintage.

_____ (1894/1981). *Capital. A Critique of Political Economy.* Volume Three. New York: Vintage.

_____ (1974a). *The Revolutions of 1848. Political Writings.* Volume I. New York: Vintage.

_____ (1974b). *Surveys From Exile. Political Writings.* Volume II. New York: Vintage.

_____ (1974c). *The Ethnological Notebooks of Karl Marx.* Assen, the Netherlands: Van Gorcum.

Marx, Karl, and Frederick Engels. (1845-1846/1976). *The German Ideology: Critique of Modern German Philosophy According to Its Representatives Feuerbach, B. Bauer and Stirner, and of German Socialism According to Its Various Prophets.* In *Collected Works.* Volume 5. New York: International Publishers.

_____ (1847-1848/1974). "Manifesto of the Communist Party." Pp. 62-98 in Karl Marx. *The Revolutions of 1848. Political Writings.* Volume I. New York: Vintage.

McCarthy, Thomas. (1978). *The Critical Theory of Habermas.* Cambridge, MA: The MIT Press.

McLelland, David. (1970). *Marx before Marxism.* New York: Harper and Row.

Merton, Robert K (1948/1967). Manifest and Latent Functions. In *On Theoretical Sociology. Five Essays, Old and New* (pp. 73-138). New York: Free Press.

_____ (1957). The Role-Set: Problems in Sociological Theory. *British Journal of Sociology,* 8(2), 106-120.

_____ (1968). *Social Theory and Social Structure.* New York: Free Press.

Meyers, Marcia K., and Irwin Garfinkel. (1999). Social Indicators and the Study of Inequality. *Economic Policy Review* (September), pp. 150-163.

Miller, David. (1999). *Principles of Social Justice.* Cambridge, MA: Harvard University Press.

Mitzman, Arthur. (1970). *The Iron Cage, An Historical Interpretation of Max Weber.* New York.

Morse, Chandler. (1969). *Modernization by Design. Social Change in the Twentieth Century.* Ithaca, Cornell University Press.

Münch, Richard. (1981). Talcott Parsons and the Theory of Action. I. The Structure of the Kantian Core. *American Journal of Sociology* 86, pp. 709-739.

Nozick, Robert (1974). *Anarchy, State and Utopia.* New York: Basic Books.

Oakes, Guy. (1982). Methodological Ambivalence: The Case of Max Weber. *Social Research,* 49, pp. 589-615.

_____ (1988a). Rickert's Value Theory and the Foundations of Weber's Methodology. *Sociological Theory* 6(1), pp. 38-51.

_____ (1988b). On Rickert's Solution to the Problem of Values. *Sociological Theory,* 6(2), pp. 263-264.

Parsons, Talcott. (1932). Economics and Sociology: Marshall in Relation to the Thought of His Time. *Quarterly Journal of Economics* 46, 316-347.

_____ (1934a). Some Reflections on 'The Nature and Significance of Economics'. *Quarterly Journal of Economics* 48, pp. 511-545.

_____ (1934b). Sociological Elements in Economic Thought, I. *Quarterly Journal of Economics* 49, pp. 414-453.

_____ (1935). Sociological Elements in Economic Thought, II. *Quarterly Journal of Economics* 49, pp. 645-667.

_____ (1935/1991). The Place of Ultimate Values in Sociological Theory. In C. Camic (Ed.).Talcott Parsons: *The Early Essays* (pp. 231-257). Chicago: University of Chicago Press.

_____ (1937/1968). *The Structure of Social Action.* New York: Free Press.

_____ (1940/1954a). Motivation of Economic Activity. In *T. Parsons. Essays in Sociological Theory. Revised Edition* (pp. 50-68). New York: Free Press.

_____ (1940/1954b). An Analytical Approach to the Theory of Social Stratification. In *T. Parsons. Essays in Sociological Theory. Revised Edition* (pp. 69-88). New York: Free Press.

_____ (1942/1954a). Some Sociological Aspects of the Fascist Movements. In *T. Parsons. Essays in Sociological Theory. Revised Edition* (pp. 123-141). New York: Free Press.

_____ (1942/1954b). Propaganda and Social Control. in *T. Parsons. Essays in Sociological Theory. Revised Edition* (pp. 142-176). New York: Free Press.

_____ (1945/1954a). The Present Position and Prospects of Systematic Theory in Sociology. In *T. Parsons. Essays in Sociological Theory. Revised Edition* (pp. 212-237). New York: Free Press.

_____ (1945/1954b). The Problem of Controlled Institutional Change. In *T. Parsons. Essays in Sociological Theory. Revised Edition* (pp. 238-274). New York: Free Press.

_____ (1949/1954). Social Classes and Class Conflict in the Light of Recent Sociological Theory. In *T.Parsons. Essays in Sociological Theory. Revised Edition* (pp. 323-335). New York: Free Press.

_____ (1950/1954). The Prospects of Sociological Theory. In *T. Parsons. Essays in Sociological Theory. Revised Edition* (pp. 348-369). New York: Free Press.

_____ (1951). *The Social System.* New York: Free Press.

_____ (1953/1954). A Revised Analytical Approach to the Theory of Social Stratification. In *T. Parsons. Essays in Sociological Theory. Revised Edition* (pp. 386-439). New York: Free Press.

_____ (1957/1960). The Distribution of Power in American Society. In T. Parsons. *Structure and Process in Modern Society* (pp. 199-225). Glencoe: Free Press.

_____ (1958/1960b). Some Reflections on the Institutional Framework of Economic Development. In T. Parsons. *Structure and Process in Modern Society* (pp. 98-131). Glencoe: Free Press.

_____ (1959a). An Approach to Psychological Theory in Terms of the Theory of Action. In S. Koch (Ed.). *Psychology: A Study of a Science.* Vol. 3 (pp. 612-711). New York: McGraw-Hill.

_____ (1960). Some Principal Characteristics of Industrial Societies. In T. Parsons. *Structure and Process in Modern Society* (pp. 132-168). Glencoe: Free Press.

_____ (1964). Evolutionary Universals in Society. *Sociological Review*, 29(3), pp. 339-357.

_____ (1960/1967). Pattern Variables Revisited: A Response to Robert Dubin. In T. Parsons. *Sociological Theory and Modern Society* (pp. 192-219). New York: Free Press.

_____ (1961b). An Outline of the Social System. In T. Parsons et al. (Eds.). *Theories of Society. Foundations of Modern Sociological Theory* (pp. 30-79). New York: Free Press.

_____ (1963/1967a). On the Concept of Political Power. In T. Parsons. *Sociological Theory and Modern Society.* (pp. 297-354). New York: Free Press.

_____ (1963/1967b). On the Concept of Influence. In T. Parsons. *Sociological Theory and Modern Society.* (pp. 355-382). New York: Free Press.

_____ (1964/1967a). Some Reflections on the Place of Force in Social Process. In T. Parsons. *Sociological Theory and Modern Society* (pp. 264-296). New York: Free Press.

_____ (1965/1966). Full Citizenship for the Negro Americans? In T. Parsons and K. Clark (Eds.). *The Negro American* (pp. 252-291). Boston: Houghton Mifflin.

_____ (1966). *Societies. Evolutionary and Comparative Perspectives.* Englewood Cliffs: Prentice-Hall.

_____ (1968/1969). On the Concept of Value-Commitments. In T. Parsons. *Politics and Social Structure.* (pp. 439-472). New York: Free Press.

_____ (1970/1977a). Some Problems of General Theory in Sociology. In T. Parsons. *Social Systems and the Evolution of Action Theory* (pp. 229-269). New York: Free Press.

_____ (1971). *The System of Modern Societies.* Englewood Cliffs: Prentice-Hall.

_____ (1971/1977). Comparative Studies and Evolutionary Change. In T. Parsons. *Social Systems and the Evolution of Action Theory* (pp. 279-320). New York: Free Press.

_____ (1975/1977). Social Structure and the Symbolic Media of Interchange. In T. Parsons. *Social Systems and the Evolution of Action Theory* (pp. 204-228). New York: Free Press.

Parsons, Talcott, and Edward A. Shils. (1951). Values, Motives, and Systems of Action. In T. Parsons and E. Shils (Eds.). *Toward a General Theory of Action* (pp. 47-275). Cambridge, MA: Harvard University Press.

Parsons, Talcott, Robert F. Bales, and Edward A. Shils. (1953). *Working Papers in the Theory of Action.* Glencoe: Free Press.

Parsons, Talcott and Robert F. Bales. (1955). *Family, Socialization and Interaction Process.*

Glencoe: Free Press.

Parsons, Talcott and Neil J. Smelser. (1956). *Economy and Society. A Study in the Integration of Economic and Social Theory*. New York: Free Press.

Parsons, Talcott and Gerald M. Platt. (1973). *The American University*. Cambridge: Harvard University Press.

Pateman, Carole. (1970). *Participation and Democratic Theory*. London: Cambridge University Press.

Pickering, W.S.F. (1984). *Durkheim's Sociology of Religion. Themes and Theories*. London: Routlage & Kegan Paul.

Polanyi, Karl. (1944). *The Great Transformation*. Boston: Beacon Hill.

Pope, Whitney, Jere Cohen, and Lawrence E. Hazelrigg. (1975). On Divergence of Weber and Durkheim: A Critique of Parsons' Convergence Thesis. *American Sociological Review*, 40, pp. 417-427.

Popper. Karl. (1944/1962). *The Open Society and its Enemies*. New York. Harper and Row.

_____ (1968). *The Logic of Scientific Discovery*. 3d ed. London: Hutchinson.

Portis, Edward Bryan. (1980). Political Action and Social Science: Max Weber's Two Arguments for Objectivity *Polity*, 12(3), 409-427.

_____ (1986). *Max Weber and Political Commitment: Science, Politics and Personality*. Philadelphia: Temple University Press.

Radcliffe-Brown, Alfred R. (1935/1952). *Structure and Function in Primitive Society*. New York: Free Press.

Rand, Ayn (1964). *The Virtue of Selfishness*. New York: New American Library.

Rawls, John. (1999). *A Theory of Justice. Revised Edition*. Cambridge, MA: Harvard University Press.

Richard, Gaston. (1975). Dogmatic atheism in the sociology of religion. In W.S.F. Pickering (Ed.). *Durkheim on Religion. A Selection of Readings with Bibliographies and Introductory Remarks* (pp. 228-276). London: Routlage & Kegan Paul.

Rickert, Heinrich. (1962). *Science and History*. Princeton: Van Nostrand.

Ricoeur, Paul. (1976). *Interpretation Theory: Discourse and the Surplus of Meaning*. Fort Worth: Texas Christian Press.

Rock, Paul. (1976). Some Problems of Interpretive Historiography. *British Journal of Sociology*, 27(3), 353-369.

Rose, Fred (1997). Toward a Class-Cultural Theory of Social Movements: Reinterpreting New Social Movements. *Sociological Forum*, 12(3), pp. 461-494.

Schedrovitsky, G. P. (1971). Configuration as a method of construction of complex knowledge. *Systematics*. Vol. 8. No 4.

Schmid, Michael. (1982). Habermas' Theory of Social Evolution. Pp. 162-180 in J. Thompson and D. Hell (eds), *Habermas: Critical Debates*. Cambridge, MA: MIT Press.

Schumpeter, Joseph A. (1074). *Capitalism, Socialism and Democracy*. New York: Harper & Row.

Schoenfeld, Eugen and Stjepan G. Meštrović. (1989). Durkheim's Concept of Justice and Its Relationship to Social Solidarity. *Sociological Analysis*, 50(2).

Schwinn, Thomas. (1998). False Connections: Systems and Action Theories in Neofunctionalism and in Jurgen Habermas. *Sociological Theory*, 16(1), pp. 75-95.

Seidman, Steven. (1984). The Main Aim and Thematic Structures of Weber's Sociology, *Canadian Journal of Sociology* 9 (Fall), pp. 82-104.

_____ (1985). The Historicist Controversy: A Critical Review with a Defense of a Revised Presentism. *Sociological Theory*, 3(1), pp. 13-16.

Simey, T.S, (1966) "Max Weber: Man of Affairs or Theoretical Sociologist?" *Sociological Review* 14, pp. 303-328.

Simmel, Georg. (1950). *The Sociology of Georg Simmel. Translated, edited and with an introduction by Kurt H. Wolff.* New York: Free Press.

_____ (1971). *On Individuality and Social Forms.* Chicago: University of Chicago Press.

Skocpol, Theda. (1996). Unraveling from Above. *The American Prospect.* No. 25 (March-April), pp. 20-25.

Smelser, Neil J. and Richard Swedberg (Editors). (1994). *Handbook of Economic Sociology.* Russel Sage Foundation.

Smikun, Emanuel. (2000). Timeless Moral Imperatives in Causal Analysis of Social Functioning. *Electronic Journal of Sociology,* 5 (1).

_____ (2005). Valuable Objects and Their Differentiation in Social Space and Time. *Fast Capitalism,* 1 (1).

Sommers, Christina Hoff (1995). *Who Stole Feminism? How Women Have Betrayed Women.* New York: Simon & Schuster.

Sørensen, Aage B. (2001). Basic Concepts of Stratification Research: Class, Status, and Power. In D. B. Grusky (Ed.). *Social Stratification: Class, Race and Gender in Sociological Perspective.* (2nd ed.). (pp. 287-300). Boulder, CO: Westview.

Sorokin, Pitirim A. (1927/1959). *Social and Cultural Mobility.* New York: Free Press.

_____ (1947). *Society, Culture and Personality: Their Structure and Dynamics. A System of General Sociology.* New York: Harper and Brothers.

Stigler, George J. (1954). The Economist Plays with Blocs. *The American Economic Review,* Vol. 44, No. 2 (May), pp. 7-14.

Swedberg, Richard (1991). Major Traditions of Economic Sociology. Annual Review of Sociology, vol. 21, pp. 251-276.

Tarascio, Vincent J. (1973). The Pareto Law of Income Distribution. *Social Science Quarterly,* 54, pp. 525-533.

Tenbruck, Friedrich H. (1980). The Problem of Thematic Unity in the Works of Max Weber. *British Journal of Sociology*, Vol. 31, No. 3, (Sep.), pp. 316-351. London: Blackwell.

Therborn, Göran. (2002). Class Perspectives: Shrink or Widen? *Acta Sociologica* No 3.

Tobin, James. (1974). Galbraith Redux. *The Yale Law Journal,* Vol. 83, No. 6 (May), pp. 1291-1303.

Tolman, Edward C. (1951). A Psychological Model. In T. Parsons and E. Shils (Eds.). *Toward a General Theory of Action.* (pp. 277-361). Cambridge, MA: Harvard University Press.

Touraine, Alain. (1981). *The Voice and the Eye: An Analysis of Social Movements.* Cambridge: Cambridge University Press.

Ultee, Wout C. (1996). Do Rational Choice Approaches Have Problems? *European Sociological Review,* 12(2), pp. 167-179.

van Gennep, A. (1975). Review. 'Les Formes élémentaires de la vie religieuse'. In W.S.F. Pickering (Ed.). *Durkheim on Religion. A Selection of Readings with Bibliographies and Introductory Remarks* (pp. 205-208). London: Routlage & Kegan Paul.

Vanlaningham, Jody; Johnson, David R and Amato, Paul. (2001). Marital Happiness, Marital Duration, and the U-Shaped Curve: Evidence from a Five-Wave

Panel Study. *Social Forces*, 78(4), pp. 1313-1341.

Vanneman, Reeve and Lynn Weber cannon (1987). *The American Perception of Class.* Philadelphia: Temple University Press.

Veenhoven, Ruut. (1996). Developments in Satisfaction-Research. Social Indicators Research 37(1), pp. 1-46.

Vogt, Evon Z. (1960). On the Concepts of Structure and Process in Cultural Anthropology. *American Anthropologist*, New Series, Vol. 62, No. 1 (Feb), pp. 18-33.

Wagner, Gerhard, and Heinz Zipprian. (1988). The Problem of Values and the Problem of Truth. *Sociological Theory*, 6(2), pp. 262-263.

Wagner, Helmut R. (1978). Between Ideal Type and Surrender: Field Research as Asymmetrical Relation. *Human Studies*, 1(2), pp. 153-164.

Wallace, Walter L. (1990). Rationality, human nature, and society in Weber's theory. *Theory and Society*, 19, pp. 199-223.

Wallwork, Ernest. (1985). Durkheim's Early Sociology of Religion. *Sociological Analysis*, 46(3), 201-217.

Walzer, Michael. (1983). *Spheres of Justice: A Defense of Pluralism and Equality.* New York: Basic Books.

Warner, W. Lloyd, Marchia Meeker, Kenneth Eells (1949). *Social class in America: A manual of procedure for the measurement of social status.* Chicago: Science Research Associates.

Weber, Marianne. (1975). *Max Weber: A Biography.* New York: John Wiley.

Weber, Max. (1896/1976). The Social Causes of the Decline of Ancient Civilization. In M. Weber. *The Agrarian Sociology of Ancient Civilizations* (pp. 387-411). London: Humanities Press.

_____ (1897-1909/1976). *The Agrarian Sociology of Ancient Civilizations.* London: Humanities Press.

_____ (1903-1907/1975). *Roscher and Knies: The Logical Problems of Historical Economics.* New York: Free Press.

_____ (1904/1949). 'Objectivity' in Social Science and Social Policy. In E. Shils and H. Finch (Eds., Trans.). *The Methodology of the Social Sciences* (pp. 49-112). New York: Free Press.

_____ (1904-1920/1958). *The Protestant Ethic and the Spirit of Capitalism.* New York: Scribner's.

_____ (1906/1949). Critical Studies in the Logic of the Cultural Sciences. In E. Shils and H. Finch (Eds.). Trans.). *The Methodology of the Social Sciences* (pp. 113-187). New York: Free Press.

_____ (1906/1978). The Logic of Historical Explanation. in W. Runciman (Ed.). *Max Weber: Selections in translation* (pp. 111-131). Cambridge, MA: Cambridge University Press.

_____ (1907/1977). *Critique of Stammler.* New York: Free Press.

_____ (1908/1971). *Methodological Introduction for the Survey of the Society for Social Policy.* In J.E.T. Eldridge (Ed.). *Max Weber: The Interpretation of Social Reality* (pp. 103-155). New York: Shoken.

_____ (1913/1981). Some Categories of Interpretive Sociology. *Sociological Quarterly*, 22(2), pp. 151-180.

_____ (1914/1949). The Meaning of 'Ethical Neutrality' in Sociology and Economics. In E. Shils and H. Finch (Eds., Trans.). *The Methodology of the*

Social Sciences (pp. 1-47). New York: Free Press.

_____ (1914/1978). Value-judgments in Social Sciences. In W. Runciman (Ed.). *Max Weber: Selections in Translation* (pp. 69-98). Cambridge, MA: Cambridge University Press.

_____ (1915/1946a). The Social Psychology of the World Religions. In H. Gerth and C. W. Mills (Eds.). *From Max Weber: Essays in Sociology* (pp. 267-301). New York: Oxford University Press.

_____ (1915/1946b). Religious Rejections of the World and Their Directions. In H. Gerth and C. W. Mills (Eds.). *From Max Weber: Essays in Sociology* (pp. 323-359). New York: Oxford University Press.

_____ (1917/1946). Science as a Vocation. In H. Gerth and C. W. Mills (Eds.). *From Max Weber: Essays in Sociology* (pp. 129-158). New York: Oxford University Press.

_____ (1919/1946). Politics as a Vocation. In H. Gerth and C. W. Mills (Eds.). *From Max Weber: Essays in Sociology* (pp. 77-128). New York: Oxford University Press.

_____ (1919-1920/1961). *General Economic History.* New York: Collier Books.

_____ (1922/1978). *Economy and Society. An Outline of Interpretive Sociology.* Berkeley, CA: University of California Press.

_____ (1924/1971). Socialism. In J.E.T. Eldridge (Ed.). *Max Weber: The Interpretation of Social Reality* (pp. 191-219). New York: Shoken.

_____ (1958). *The Protestant Ethic and the Spirit of Capitalism.* New York: Charles Scribner's Sons.

_____ (1972). Simmel as a Sociologist. *Social Research,* 39(1), pp. 155-163.

Wessel Jr., Leonard P. (1979). *Karl Marx: Romantic Irony and the Proletariat. The Mythopoetic Origins of Marxism.* Baton Rouge: Louisiana State University Press.

Whimster, Sam. (1980). The Profession of History in the Work of Max Weber: Its Origins and Limitations. *British Journal of Sociology,* 31(3), pp. 352-376.

Wickens, Thomas (1989). *Multidimensional Contingency Tables Analysis in the Social Sciences.* Hillsdale: Lawrence Erlbaum.

Wright, Erik Olin. (2002). The Shadow of Exploitation in Weber's Class Analysis. *American Sociological Review,* Vol. 67, No. 6 (Dec.), pp. 832-853.

Zafirovski, Milan. (1999). Economic Sociology in Retrospect and Prospect. *American Journal of Economics and Sociology.* October.

_____(2001). Reexamining Economic Sociology: Beyond Rational Choice Reductionism. *The American Sociologist,* vol. 32(1), pp. 78-99.

_____(2006). Parsonian Economic Sociology: Bridges to Contemporary Economics. *American Journal of Economics and Sociology,* vol. 65(1), pp. 75-108.

Zaret, David. (1980). From Weber to Parsons and Schutz: The Eclipse of History in Modern Social Theory. *American Journal of Sociology,* Vol. 85, No. 5 (Mar.), pp. 1180-1201.

Zukin, Sharon and Paul DiMaggio (Editors). (1990). *Structures of Capital: The Social Organization of the Economy.* Cambridge University Press.